HOW TO PRAY FOR PEOPLE

AND LEAD THEM TO JESUS

By Name

BRIAN ALARID

PRAISE FOR **BY NAME**

"Two things that are obvious about Brian Alarid are that he is passionate about Jesus and prayer. You can't be around him long before you catch his enthusiasm. You won't be able to read this book and not feel an urgency to take your praying to another level and to tell someone about Jesus!"

—Richard Blackaby
Author, *Experiencing God, The Ways of God*

"In his book, *By Name*, Brian Alarid outlines a simple model for sharing the good news that every one of us can follow! Pulling on stirring stories from his own remarkable life, Brian shows that if we engage with people on a personal level, the love of Jesus will break through and change hearts! By following the advice laid out in *By Name*, we can begin to impact lives using the same strategy Jesus used during His ministry. If you love people and pray—you need to read *By Name!"*

—Dave Ferguson
Lead Visionary, NewThing, Author, *B.L.E.S.S. 5 Everyday Ways to Love Your Neighbor and Change the World*

"Brian Alarid, with his infectious vision for every person on the globe, invites us to join him. This is an invitation into God's tenderest intention that every person on the planet encounters Him who created them and woos them through each of us. Commit yourself to join us."

—Dr. Mac Pier
Founder, Movement.Org, Lausanne Co-Catalyst for Cities

"*By Name* by Brian Alarid is a powerful book that will challenge you to pray for every person by name and share your faith with them. This book will show you how to befriend people far from God and impact them for eternity. If you want to see God's Kingdom grow faster than ever, read this book!"

—Samuel Rodriguez
Lead Pastor of New Season, President of NHCLC,
Author of *Your Mess, God's Miracle!*

"John Wesley stated: 'God does nothing but in answer to prayer.' If that is even partially true, we have a monumental task ahead of us. Our vision at Empowered21 is 'that every person on Earth will have an authentic encounter with Jesus Christ through the power and presence of the Holy Spirit by Pentecost 2033.' These encounters will only happen as a result of prayer, which means we are called to pray for every person on Earth. In his new book, Brian Alarid mixes inspirational accounts of praying for individuals by name with a bold strategic global vision that will inspire all of us to pray for everyone *by name*."

—Dr. Billy Wilson
Chair of Empowered21 and the Pentecostal World Fellowship, and President of Oral Roberts University

"My dear brother Brian has written this book from deep personal experience and a life dedicated to prayer that embraces the power and principles of prayer that cover one person as well as the whole world. Brian's heart for prayer for every individual mirrors Father God's heart for each person alive on earth. The connection between the global move of God in the world and the individual power of prayer is made so poignantly clear in this book and in the life of its author, more than in any book I have read, and more than any person I have met. I pray that this book will stir up the passion and practice of prayer in the individual believer, the Church and prayer movements worldwide as it has done in my life."

—Goodwill Shana
Board Chair, World Evangelical Association (WEA)
President, Association Of Evangelicals In Africa (AEA)
Co-Chair, Empowered21 Africa Cabinet

"If you are going to write a book on prayer, then it follows you ought to be a man devoted to prayer yourself. And Brian Alarid is such a man. Rarely have I met a man as determined as Brian when it comes to mobilizing God's people to pray. He burns with this passion, and it just oozes through the pages of this book. I love this man and all he represents."

—Yang Tuck Yoong
Chairman, The Alliance of Pentecostal & Charismatic Churches in Singapore, Senior Pastor, Cornerstone Community Church

"When it comes to books on prayer, I tend to enjoy the classics. Chadwick, Murray, and Bounds far outweigh much modern-day fair when it comes to both spiritual gravitas and depth of insight. Brian Alarid has written an instant classic. In a Christian culture where prayer is often viewed as a magic wand to get stuff from God, Brian awakens his readers to the centrality of prayer in the process of evangelism. *By Name* not only inspires us to *intercede* for the lost people we know, but it also equips us to *intervene* in their lives by being used by God to share the Gospel in a loving, relational way. This book has the potential to change the world and rock yours in the process."

—Greg Stier
Founder and Visionary, Dare 2 Share

"This book is a must-read! The prayer movement across the Earth is growing rapidly. One of the most important parts of this is that we pray for everyone by name, beginning with our close circle of relatives and friends. Brian Alarid is at the front of this movement. He unpacks his own journey in an easy-to-read way, including powerful and personal stories. As you read this book, I believe you will receive an impartation from God that will give new meaning to your daily life."

—Mark Anderson
YWAM and call2all

"Prayer is the key to global connectivity, which is one of the keys to release the Collective Might of the Church. Brian and Mercy have been leaders in the effort to unite the Church in prayer for the world, one person at a time, one name at a time. What an important idea and an important book. Grateful for this essential work."

—Scott and Theresa Beck
Co-founders, Gloo

"If you want a miracle you must begin with an impossibility! Brian Alarid's timely challenge, *By Name,* beckons God's people globally to unite in turning a mammoth impossibility into a majestic miracle. Praying for every person in the world *by name* will truly be a miracle for the ages! Read it! Believe it! Live it! It's your invitation to be a part of history's great, end-time harvest.

—Dick Eastman
Every Home for Christ, Author, *The Hour that Changes the World*

"I love this book! So practical, so compelling, so biblical! Brian shares with us real-life stories that encourage a simple prayer strategy—praying for people by name! Praying for people *By Name* will ignite your heart to share your faith with them! I believe God will use this book to foster a mighty Christ—awakening in the nations of the earth!"

—Jason Hubbard
Director, International Prayer Connect

I recall sitting at a global leaders' meeting where Brian Alarid was present. We had not met previously. He struck me as an unassuming "nice guy," but as he was introduced as the director of World Prays and began to share, I was transfixed, not by his charisma (although he definitely has some), but by the power of the vision he carried with humble authenticity. That day, I met someone who would challenge and inspire me to believe God for "above and beyond" outcomes—more than I could have imagined alone. *By Name* is a must-read message to today's church of what it means to be true followers of Jesus who intentionally pray for others and lead them to Him.

—David Wells
General Superintendent, The Pentecostal Assemblies of Canada

I dedicate this book to my friend, mentor,
and spiritual father, Dick Eastman.

Thirty-one years ago, I read your book,
The Hour That Changes The World,
and it changed my life. I prayed a simple prayer,
"Lord, I pray that one day I could meet
Dick Eastman, and maybe he would lay
his hands on me and pray for me."

Little did I know then that you would become the greatest
influence in my life. Beyond the billions of people God has
impacted through you, what stands out to me is your humility,
consistency in prayer, and devotion to Jesus.

Thank you for believing in me, praying for me
and with me, encouraging me, mentoring me,
and being a spiritual father to me.
This book and the movement it chronicles
wouldn't be possible without you.

I love you, honor you, and cherish you.

Your spiritual son,
Brian

ACKNOWLEDGEMENTS

I want to honor the person who was the inspiration behind this book. **Jesus**, You are my Lord, my Savior, and my first love. All this is because of You and for You.

Mercy, you are the love of my life and my best friend. I am nothing without you. You and me to the end!

Chloe, Colin, and Lauren, you are the greatest gifts God has ever given me. No father has ever been prouder of his children. I love you, adore you, and treasure you.

Mart Green, thank you for your friendship, mentorship, and support. Thank you for believing in me and chasing this crazy dream with me. Love you, friend!

Mark Anderson, thank you for sharing with me the vision God gave you to pray for every person by name and allowing me to run with it. I honor you!

Pray For All Global Leadership Council, it is a joy and privilege to do life and ministry with you.

Holden Hill, thank you for helping me write my story and express the passion and vision inside my heart so eloquently.

Anna McHargue, thank you for editing this book and bringing your expertise to this project.

CONTENTS

"But now thus says the LORD, he who created you,
O Jacob, he who formed you, O Israel:
'Fear not, for I have redeemed you;
I have called you by name, you are mine.'"[1]

Isaiah 43:1

FOREWORD BY
RICK WARREN

Like all great revolutionary concepts, this book presents an idea that is:

simple (everyone can understand it),
scalable (everyone can do it), and,
sustainable (every pastor and church can support it).

If each follower of Christ on earth will commit to using the simple strategies that Brian explains in this book, not only will every unbeliever be prayed for by name, but they will also get to hear a personal witness of the Good News before the 2000th birthday of the Church on Pentecost Sunday, 2033.

If you study church history, you will see a repeatable pattern: One of the clearest signs that God is at work, preparing *his church* for a new wave of *revitalization* and preparing *his world* for a new wave of *evangelization* is when followers of Christ in different parts of the world start acting on the same idea – without knowing each other! Only the Spirit of God can make that happen.

As I've traveled and trained Christian leaders in 164 nations, I've been astounded to see firsthand this new groundswell of interest in praying for unbelievers *BY NAME!*

For years we have heard about *the numbers* of people in each nation who don't know Jesus. But with today's

i

technology we can now know *their names!* This allows our prayers for their salvation to be more personal, passionate, and powerful.

Finishing the Task is the largest coalition of Christians, churches, denominations, and agencies around the world collaborating to complete the Great Commission that Jesus assigned to us. Jesus' last instructions must be our first priority! Specifically, Finishing the Task partners have agreed on 4 "B" goals to be completed by 2033:

Bibles: that everyone on earth has access to a Bible in their own heart language. This will require Bible distribution, Bible engagement, and Bible translation.

Believers: that every believer on earth is trained to share the different ways that Jesus has changed their life so that every unbeliever gets to hear a personal witness of the Good News.

Bodies of Christ: that everyone on earth has access to a local church for spiritual support. Tens of millions of new churches must be started in homes and businesses around the world.

Breakthrough Prayer: that every unbeliever on earth gets prayed for *by name*—for their salvation, between now and Pentecost Sunday, 2033.

As the global chairman of the *Finishing the Task* coalition, I am grateful to Brian for writing this helpful book, and I am excited to endorse *BY NAME* as a recommended resource for the Breakthrough Prayer and Believers goals.

Study this book. Then do it! Then buy a hundred more copies to share with others. May God bless and use you for his purposes in your generation.

—Dr. Rick Warren

Global Chairman, Finishing the Task Coalition
Author, *The Purpose Driven Life & Purpose Driven Church*
Co-founder, Celebrate Recovery
Chancellor, Spurgeon's College, London
https://finishingthetask.com

A MESSAGE FROM
DAVID WELLS

A deeply appreciated gift of my calling and role is to sit at national and global tables where you are introduced to persons who challenge and inspire you to believe God for "above and beyond" outcomes – more than you could have imagined alone.

I recall the first time I sat at a global meeting table with Brian Alarid. He was unassuming, a "nice guy," but I wasn't really sure why he was there. Dr. William Wilson, chair of both the Pentecostal World Fellowship and the Empowered21 network, introduced him to the table as the director of World Prays. As Brian shared I was transfixed, not by his charisma (although he definitely has some), but by the power of the vision he shared with humble authenticity.

Brian clearly communicated that in our shared vision to see "Everyone" receive the good news of Jesus' redeeming and transforming work of grace by Pentecost 2033, we also need to recognize the importance of a shared initiative to see every person on the planet prayed for "by name" by 2033. The reminder was powerfully given that prayer, spiritual life, and empowerment are absolutely linked to sharing the transforming message of Jesus to our "Ones" and to everyone in their multiple contexts. Encapsulated in that call is that every church would be a "house of prayer for all nations."

The simply stated goal of this book is to pray for people and lead them to Jesus. *"By Name"* leads us to the understanding that if we are praying for our "Ones" by name then we must also be participants in seeing them come to Jesus as we adopt five lifestyle habits that Jesus modeled. These can be summarized by the acronym B.L.E.S.S.:

- *Begin with Prayer*
- *Listen to Them*
- *Eat with Them*
- *Serve Them*
- *Share Jesus with Them*

This is what a lifestyle of relational evangelism truly looks like. Intercession intersects with incarnation and proclamation to bring transformation to individuals, regions, and nations.

As followers of Jesus, there are many aspects to our whole-hearted, whole-minded, whole-life discipleship, both personally and corporately. Worship, unity, engaging God's Word, and other disciplines and practices are important aspects of being the people of God. To complement these, we invite you to read this book, and then personally and as ministries ponder and pray how *By Name* will be applied in the contexts you serve in.

We, as a Spirit-empowered family of ministries and churches, are committed to do our part to fulfill the mission Jesus has called us to as we work together in unity with sisters and brothers globally to see "Everyone" receive a Spirit-empowered, embodied presentation of the good news of Jesus Christ. I am grateful that we have *By Name* to inspire and equip us as we fulfill that call.

For Him,

David Wells
General Superintendent,
The Pentecostal Assemblies of Canada

David.Wells@paoc.org

AUTHOR'S NOTE

I accepted the call to lead the initiative to pray for every person in the world *by name* after a conversation with my friend, Mark Anderson, in Brazil in October 2019.

The vision began taking shape, and we were gaining momentum, but I knew I needed a team. And not just any team, but the ultimate dream team that could help us complete this impossible task. The Holy Spirit, as usual, was already innumerable steps ahead of me.

On May 13, 2020, I received a phone call from my friend Mart Green. He is the Chief Investment Officer at Hobby Lobby, a privately owned chain of over 1,000 retail stores in the United States.

"I believe the Bible movement and the prayer movement need to come together at some point," Mart said in his signature upbeat tone.

"But first," Mart continued, "I believe the prayer movements need to come together. What do you think could unite all the different prayer movements?"

I didn't need to think long about my answer. It was the only thing on my mind lately.

"Maybe the vision of praying for all people in 1 Timothy 2:1-6 could bring together different movements and denominations to accomplish something greater than any of us could on our own." As Mart and I unpacked this vision of praying for everyone by name, the Holy Spirit lit up our hearts. Our excitement was tangible.

"I love it!" Mart said. "Let's build a team and chase it."

We had no idea how we would pull it off, but that was God's job—our job was simply to obey God. As Dr. Martin Luther King Jr. said, "Take the first step in faith. You don't have to see the whole staircase, just take the first step." [2]

So we took the first step, even though we couldn't see the second step. As Bob Wiley would say, "Baby steps… baby steps." [3]

Mart and I huddled over a Zoom call a few days later with Dick Eastman, David Ferguson, Kathy Branzell, and Dave Butts—four of America's most respected prayer leaders. A week later, I presented our vision to Scott Beck and Jeff Fray at Gloo. Scott and Jeff are technology gurus, and they loved the idea.

"So, basically," Scott said, "you want to pray for eight billion people who live in 200 different countries and speak 6,000 languages. And somehow, learn their names and pray for them by name? That's like the largest data project in history!"

"I know it's crazy, Scott, but this was God's idea, not mine!"

Scott flashed a smile, and his eyes glinted with excitement. "Alright, I'm in."

We were building momentum. God was opening doors, people were jumping in, and the engine was warming up. A few days later, I received a phone call from Ashley Wilson and Dr. Billy Wilson, the President of Oral Roberts University and Chairman of Empowered21. It was this call that kicked this vision into fifth gear.

"God has given Empowered21 a vision that every person on Earth would have an authentic encounter with Jesus Christ through the power and presence of the Holy Spirit... by Pentecost 2033," Dr. Wilson said.[4]

"Praying for everyone by name is an essential part of that. I want you to lead that charge and help us build a global prayer alliance." God had placed the same burden on his heart as mine.

But being the visionary that he is, Dr. Wilson upped the ante yet further. Not only were we going to pray for every person on the planet by name, but we were committing to do so by Pentecost 2033.

That was taking impossible by the horns and riding it straight into insanity. But as the legendary author Napoleon Hill wrote, "A 'goal' is a dream with a deadline."[5] We may not finish this task by 2033—only God knows—but if we don't put a deadline on it, we will never make progress toward it.

Seemingly all at once, leaders all around the world were receiving the same download from the Holy Spirit to pray for everyone by name. I couldn't help but think about what French novelist Victor Hugo wrote, "Nothing else in the world...not all the armies...is so powerful as an idea whose time has come."[6]

Indeed, praying for everyone by name was an idea whose time had come. Since then, week by week and month by month, the Father has continued to expand our global team.

My friend Samuel Rodriguez told me, "Brian, we have been praying for people for centuries. But praying for people by name, now that's next level. That's the difference between a 4G and a 5G network. A 5G network is 100 times faster than a 4G network. That's how praying for every person by name will impact the growth of God's Kingdom! Count me in!"

Soon, we coined a name for the movement that fit our vision like a hand-in-glove: Pray For All.

I felt immensely honored to be part of the team we were building, but at the same time, I felt utterly unqualified to lead it. I needed someone more experienced than me to give leadership to this movement, and I knew exactly who to ask.

I drove to Colorado Springs to pray with my spiritual father, Dick Eastman, and asked him if he would serve as the chairman of Pray For All.

Dick looked into my eyes and said, "Brian, God gave me the vision to pray for every nation by name, but he's given you the vision to pray for every person by name. This is your time to lead, and I will support you." Dick laid his hands on me and anointed me for the journey ahead.

I wish I could say that I've never doubted or second-guessed God and the vision He's given us, but you would instantly call my bluff. I often feel insufficient, unqualified, and incapable. I know I don't have what it takes to accomplish this.

But I remind myself that this vision didn't come from me, Mark, Billy, Dick, or any other human being. It came from the heart of God for the body of Christ worldwide and in every generation. He shared it with the Apostle Paul, who recorded it in the Scriptures for posterity.

In October 2022, I presented the vision of Pray For All at Finishing The Task (FTT) with Rick Warren. My friend, Jason Hubbard, who leads the prayer team for Finishing The Task, adopted Pray For All as one of FTT's global prayer initiatives.

A few days later, I had dinner at a Brazilian steakhouse in Houston with my friend Dr. Master Oboletswe Matlhaope, the General Secretary of the Association of Evangelicals in Africa. Master said, "Brian, I want to make Pray For All the official prayer strategy of the AEA. Can you imagine what would happen if 1.2 billion Africans were prayed for by name?"

In June 2023, I will join Billy Wilson and Rick Warren and thousands of leaders in Amsterdam to launch the *Everyone* campaign—an initiative to reach every person on the planet with the Gospel by Pentecost 2033. This will be a defining moment in church history as the global body of Christ unites for the greatest decade of prayer, evangelism, and church planting in history (Amsterdam2023.com).

Over the past three years, we have built regional hubs in Austin, Texas, Guatemala, South Africa, Kenya, Singapore, India, Sri Lanka, and Nepal to pioneer this initiative and contextualize it.

In the past eighteen months, we have prayed for over 500 million people by name through the efforts of our partners. God has blessed us with incredible partners like call2all, Empowered21, Finishing The Task, Cru, Run Ministries, Movement Day, New Thing, International Prayer Connect, Dare 2 Share, Every Home For Christ, Bless Every Home,

Go Movement, Gloo, the Association of Evangelicals in Africa, One Hope, Great Commandment Network, Prayer Covenant, and many, many more.

You have a piece in this global movement as well. Whether you are a believer, pastor, intercessor, or movement leader—we need you. We can't pray for everyone without you. Your prayer, mobilization, and evangelism efforts matter to God's global mission.

May God use you in astounding ways as you say *yes* to Him and begin praying for people by name and sharing Jesus with them using the B.L.E.S.S. lifestyle explained in this book. All for the glory of our risen Savior, Jesus!

Brian Alarid

INTRODUCTION

We've heard them before and might hear them again: "That's impossible!" Two words that every dreamer has to face at some point. But there are people for whom those words were not terminal but seminal to what they accomplished. Look at the "impossibles" they overcame:

"Well-informed people know it is impossible to transmit the voice over wires and that were it possible to do so, the thing would be of no practical value."[7] — An editorial in the Boston Post, 1865. Today, over 6.9 billion people have a smartphone, so apparently, the phone is of some value.[8]

"Flight by machines heavier than air is unpractical and insignificant, if not impossible."[9]—Simon Newcomb, Director of the U.S. Naval Observatory, 1902. A year later, Orville and Wilbur Wright achieved the first powered, sustained, and controlled airplane flight in Kitty Hawk, North Carolina. Airplanes transport 2.8 billion passengers per year.[10] Sounds practical and significant to me!

"There is not the slightest indication that [nuclear energy] will ever be obtainable. It would mean that the atom would have to be shattered at will." [11]— Albert Einstein, one of the greatest physicists of all time, 1932. Only nineteen years later, nuclear energy was generated from a reactor.

"I think there is a world market for maybe five computers."[12] — Thomas Watson, chairman of IBM, 1943. There are over 2 billion computers today.[13] I'd call that a great market.

INTRODUCTION

Until sixty-nine years ago, no athlete in history had ever run a mile in less than four minutes. Breaking that barrier was thought to be impossible, but a British runner named Roger Bannister ran the mile at Oxford in three minutes and 59.4 seconds on May 6, 1954.[14]

You would think Roger's record would stand for decades or at least years. But that's not what happened. Bannister's record lasted only *forty-six* days!

Since that barrier-breaking day, over 1,600 athletes have done what Roger did. Less than four minutes has become the standard for middle-distance runners. When one person breaks through the impossible, the impossible becomes possible for others.

What's your *impossible*?

Maybe you've been told you will never get out of debt.

Never own your own home.

Never heal from your sickness.

Never be able to have children.

Never lose weight.

Never overcome depression.

Never start a business.

Never earn your degree.

Never find true love.

But don't forget that you serve a God who specializes in doing the impossible. Jesus said in Matthew 19:26, *"With man this is impossible, but with God all things are possible!"*

Boxing legend Muhammad Ali once said, "Impossible is just a big word thrown around by small men who find it easier to live in the world they've been given than to explore the power they have to change it. Impossible is not a fact. It's an opinion. Impossible is not a declaration. It's a dare. Impossible is potential. Impossible is temporary. Impossible is nothing."[15]

I know how daunting it can be to look at an impossible challenge and decide to chase it even though you are scared to death. When my friend Mark Anderson shared that impossible vision with me a few years ago: "Brian, I believe God wants us to pray for every person in the world *by name* and share the Gospel with them," I nodded politely, trying to conceal my skepticism, but I thought, *You want to pray for every person in the world by name—all eight billion of them? That's impossible!*

You're probably thinking the same thing. How would we ever be able to identify every person in the world, know their names, and pray for them? How could anyone rally such a vast army of intercessors to pray for them and share the Gospel with them?

Then Mark added, "And you know what else? I believe God has chosen *you* to lead that charge."

The vision was huge and compelling, but how would we ever accomplish it, and why would we even attempt such a far-fetched thing? I had more questions than answers. But as time went on, this vision wouldn't leave me alone.

In October 2019, I found myself with Mark again in the back row of a twelve-seat passenger van stuck in Rio de Janeiro's bumper-to-bumper traffic. We had just finished a conference with Loren Cunningham, Paul Eshleman, Dave Gibson, and David Hamilton.

"Hey Brian, we can't reach everyone with the Gospel without first praying for them," Mark said. He looked me right in the eye and went straight for my jugular.

"Are you willing to devote your life to this assignment of mobilizing prayer for everyone by name?"

A nearby car blared its horn as I chewed on Mark's words. This vision consumed me, but I had no idea how to make it a reality. It seemed impractical and unachievable.

And that's when I felt it. The gentle nudge of the Holy Spirit I know so well was stirring me to accept this assignment. I knew at that moment that I had no choice but to surrender.

"Mark, this is a crazy idea that only God could ever pull off, but I believe He has called me to be a part of it. I'm all in! Let's go for it."

A wise man once said, "The problem human beings face is not that we aim too high and fail, but that we aim too low and succeed."[16] I would rather attempt the impossible and make it halfway there than sit at home and succeed at nothing. I knew if I didn't at least try, I would regret it for the rest of my life.

As Paulo Coelho said, "Life doesn't come with any guarantees. You have to risk it to get the biscuit."[17] So I jumped out of the plane, so to speak, hoping the parachute would open. (I'm halfway down—we'll soon find out!)

Here's the point: Billions of people around the world don't know Jesus, but God has given you and me the power to change that. And it all starts with prayer. Prayer is the catalyst—the fire that ignites your heart for God's mission.

> **Billions of people around the world don't know Jesus, but God has given you and me the power to change that. And it all starts with prayer.**

You might be wondering: What does this have to do with me? How do I fit into this huge vision? I'm just one person—what difference could my prayers possibly make?

This book will inspire you to pray for people far from God, befriend them, and share your faith with them, and in so doing, impact them for eternity. Everybody can pray for somebody, and together we can pray for everybody.

Will you join me on this *impossible* adventure?

Let's go!

CHAPTER 1

THE POWER OF NAMES

*"Your name is more important than you can possibly imagine.
It's a core part of our identity, and many feel frustrated
when someone just benignly mispronounces it, as if it was an
intentional slight. This is because it is a part of who we are,
much like our culture and heritage."*[18]
— Amethyst Tagney

"What's in a name?"[19]

Centuries ago, William Shakespeare posed this timeless question. There is more to names than we probably ever realized. Let me explain what I mean. Play along with me for a moment.

Bond, James Bond.

Sherlock Holmes.

Mary Poppins.

Black Panther.

Romeo and Juliet.

Bilbo, Frodo, Samwise, and Gandalf.

Wonder Woman.

Huckleberry Finn.

Neo and Morpheus.

Nancy Drew.

Don Quixote.

Luke Skywalker and Princess Leia.

Katniss Everdeen.

Homer Simpson.

CHAPTER 1

Those are some of the most iconic fictional characters in history. My favorite is Luke Skywalker because he was loyal, a fighter for justice, and a pillar of integrity. (And I mean, come on, he had a lightsaber!)

But the name Luke Skywalker only means something to you if you have watched the *Star Wars* movies. Luke's name has meaning because of who he was and what he represents. If fictional names can evoke this much emotion, what about the names of the people we love?

A friend asked me the other day how my kids were doing. My first response was, "They're doing great!" With that answer, I could feel my general affection for them. But as I began describing how they were doing individually, a flood of emotion and memories filled my heart and mind.

When I say the name of my firstborn, *Chloe*, I think of the hundreds of hours we have spent watching our favorite shows like *24*, *Fringe*, *Blindspot*, and *Quantico*. We pause the show and dissect what just happened or predict what will happen next. Memories of teaching Chloe to lead worship when she was five, late-night Sonic dates, and sneaking Grape-Cranberry drinks and crackers into her hospital room warm my heart.

The name of my son, *Colin*, carries deep emotion with it. I remember he was born deaf and couldn't hear me say his name, but also that the Lord healed him and carried him through years of speech therapy and surgeries. I remember our trip to New York City to watch the Yankees play, and his favorite player, Aaron Judge, hit a home run. He still says it

2

was the best day of his life. And I think of all the hours spent playing basketball in our backyard or throwing the football.

The name of my third child, *Lauren*, bursts with energy, joy, and laughter in my mind. Lauren and I love eating popcorn and watching *Gilmore Girls*. We go out for Gelato and laugh at the most random stuff. I love Lauren's honey-brown eyes, and she loves my green eyes. We never need a reason to drop everything and just dance. *Alright stop, collaborate and listen.* [20]

I love all my children, but when I say their names, I'm reminded of my special love for each of them. When I say my kids' names, I am communicating that I love them individually and uniquely.

I love you, *Chloe*.

I love you, *Colin*.

I love you, *Lauren*.

Names evoke emotions, purpose, and memories. They are more than practical ways to differentiate people from others. Names hold identity, meaning, and often destiny.

Scholar Valerie Alia writes, "When you are born, you are given an identity through your name. A name helps differentiate you from others. The impact of a name on identity is intercultural. Names are always central in defining identity."[21]

> **Names evoke emotions, purpose, and memories. They hold identity, meaning, and often destiny.**

CHAPTER 1

Every Name for One Name

Good ideas come and go, but only *God ideas* last for eternity. In my journey to build a global movement to pray for everyone by name, God has often reminded me that this is His idea, not just a good idea. And it is anchored in the Scriptures.

The Apostle Paul wrote in 1 Timothy 2:1-6: *"I urge, then, first of all, that petitions, prayers, intercession, and thanksgiving be made for all people—for kings and all those in authority, that we may live peaceful and quiet lives in all godliness and holiness.*

This is good, and pleases God our Savior, who wants all people to be saved and to come to a knowledge of the truth. For there is one God and one mediator between God and mankind, the man Christ Jesus, who gave himself as a ransom for all people."

The New Living Translation says simply, *"Pray for all people."* The central theme of this passage is *all people*. The Apostle Paul makes three significant points:

Verse 1: God commands us to pray for *all people*.
Verse 3: God wants *all people* to be saved.
Verse 6: Jesus gave His life as a ransom for *all people*.

The Greek words translated as "all people" in 1 Timothy 2 are *pantōn anthrōpōn*, which mean "every human."[22] It is worthy of note that Paul didn't use the Greek word *ethne*, which refers to entire ethnic groups. That's because we are

4

saved as individuals and not as people groups. Salvation is personal and individual. People come to faith in Christ one at a time.

Inspired by the Holy Spirit, Paul lays out the challenge of praying for *all people*—every man, woman, and child. As far as I know, no generation has ever prayed *personally* for every human alive. This is an unfulfilled mandate in Scripture that we can't ignore any longer.

A rational person might shake their head and say, "I appreciate where you're coming from, but be realistic. *Every* person by name? What you mean is *most* people, right?" No. Impossible as it may sound, we believe God meant it when He said *all* people.

As I continued to seek the Lord about this vision, I asked Him to show me why this was so important to Him. He gave me a deeply personal example. God reminded me of the day our daughter Chloe was hospitalized with near-complete amnesia and could not walk or open her eyes. She didn't even know her own name. The date was May 13, 2016.

A few hours after her neurologist said Chloe would never walk again, a pastor from São Paulo reached out to me on WhatsApp. I didn't know him, but a mutual friend had shared the urgent prayer request for Chloe's healing with him, and he had mobilized several churches in Brazil to pray for her.

It meant the world to me that people were praying for Chloe when she couldn't even remember her name. They weren't praying generic prayers; they were praying for her specifically. The Lord whispered to me: "*Everyone* is my

Chloe. I want everyone prayed for by name because I love them even more than you love Chloe."

Drop. The. Mic!

As Simon Sinek says, "Your why matters."[23] The Apostle Paul says we should pray for everyone because God wants all people to be saved. That is a very compelling *why*. Paul is implying that the salvation of many people depends on our prayers.

God is waiting for a generation to arise and say, "We're in. You told us to pray for everyone, so You will help us do it." Why not *us,* and why not *now*? Why wouldn't God give us everything we need to pray for everyone by name? After all, He commanded us to do so in the Scriptures.

God is inviting you and me into His quest to save the world, and the first step is to pray for people. Prayer is a simple act, but according to this passage and many others, it has an eternal impact. Dick Eastman puts it this way: "When we get to heaven, we will realize that everyone there is a result of someone's prayer."[24]

God's love compels us to pray for eight billion people by name so they can know the only name that has the power to save them. The name that is above every other name. The name that saves sinners, calls prodigals home, heals the sick, and comforts the brokenhearted. The name that causes every demon in hell to tremble and every angel in heaven to worship. The name of…**Jesus.**

The name *Jesus* means "Savior." The angel said to Joseph in Matthew 1:21, *"She will give birth to a son, and you are to give him the name Jesus, because he will save his people from their sins.*" Jesus was given a name that described His mission and purpose in life. He was sent to Earth to become the Savior of the world.

In Ancient Rome, the predictive power of a person's name was captured by the Latin proverb *nomen est omen*, meaning "the name is a sign or the name speaks for itself."[25] We can see examples of this all around us. Usain Bolt, the famous sprinter and eight-time Olympic Champion, has truly lived up to his name.

In the Bible, names are significant because they reveal people's character and often their fate. Isaac and Rebekah named the younger of their twin sons *Jacob* because he was deceitful from the womb. He tried to grab his brother Esau's heel so he could come out first.

And sure enough, Jacob became deceitful, as his name indicated. This is a biblical example of *nomen est omen*. But what happened when Jacob wrestled with God and had a change of heart? God changed his name to *Israel* to reflect the change in his nature. Israel means "God strives."

Maybe you don't like your name, or maybe you or others equate your name to something bad. Perhaps there are stains in your past and mistakes you've made that you can't undo. But God promises to give you a *new name*—a new identity in Him.

Jesus said in Revelation 2:17: *"And I will give to each one a white stone, and on the stone will be engraved a new name that no one understands except the one who receives it."*[26] Have you noticed God has a thing for names?

Called by Name

David wrote in Psalm 147:4, *"He determines the number of the stars and calls them each by name."* Scientists estimate our observable universe contains over 200 billion trillion (called a sextillion) stars.[27] It is difficult for us to fathom how large the universe is. It's like a fly trying to understand how far it is from New York City to Dubai.

God not only found the time to create 200 sextillion stars, but He also *named* all of them. Why would He do that? Because names really matter to God. When God created the first humans, He called them *Adam* and *Eve*. They weren't merely man and woman—they had personal names and mattered to God. And then God brought all the animals to Adam so he could name them.

Kyle Hildebrant and Ryan Durant made this astute observation about naming: "Humans have a deep-seated need to name and be named…A name is more than a word. It can mean many things and take on many roles. We all bring our own associations—for good or ill…Through the act of naming, we make ties and emotional bonds with people and things."[28]

When you have a name, you have a purpose, a destiny, and a sense of value. We name just about everything we care about. We name our children, pets, and stuffed animals. Many people even name their cars and musical instruments. We name our cities, states, and nations. Alexander the Great named seventy cities after himself.

In the movie, *Cast Away*, Tom Hanks named his volleyball *Wilson* because it was the only friend he had on the deserted island. We tend to name anything important to us. When you name something, you humanize it and attach meaning and value to it.

Before your parents named you, God already named you and wrote a book about you. David wrote in Psalm 139:16, *"All the days ordained for me were written in your book before one of them came to be."* In this book, God wrote your skin tone, eye and hair color, height, personality, natural abilities, and destiny.

Have you ever wondered, *Does God really care about what I am going through? Does He see my pain and my struggles? Does He even notice me?* God said in Isaiah 49:16, *"See, I have written your name on the palms of my hands."*[29] God loves you so much that He engraved your name like a tattoo on His hand. You are special to Him, and His eyes are always upon you.

God sees you and knows you *personally*. He can spot you in a crowd of eight billion people and call your name. Just like a parent can spot their child on a busy playground full of hundreds of kids.

Last summer, I lost my daughter, Lauren, at Disney World, where over 57,000 people visit daily. I was freaking out. It took a while, but eventually, I spotted her in a crowd and screamed her name. She turned around, ran into my arms, and said, "Dad, where were you? I thought I had lost you!"

God said to His people in Isaiah 43:1, *"Fear not, for I have redeemed you; I have called you by name, you are mine."*[30] God is on a first-name basis with you—no other religious leader can make that claim. Your name evokes incredible emotion and affection in His heart. And God says you are *mine*—you belong to Him. As my friend Joel Osteen says, "Your value doesn't come because of *who* you are. It comes because of *whose* you are."[31] You are God's, and He is yours. And what's His is yours. Isn't that comforting?

Jesus said in John 10:3, *"The sheep hear his voice, and he calls his own sheep by name."* In ancient times, it was common for shepherds to name each of their sheep, much like we name our pets today.

Author Max Lucado brilliantly explains this concept: "The Shepherd knows his sheep. He knows each one by name. The Shepherd knows you. He knows your name. And He will never forget it. 'I have written your name on my hand (Isaiah 49:16).' Quite a thought, isn't it? Your name on God's hand. Your name on God's lips."[32] Your name is on God's lips and God's hand. How amazing is that?

Jesus said in Revelation 3:5, *"The one who conquers will be clothed thus in white garments, and I will never blot his name out of the book of life. I will confess his name before my Father and before his angels."*

When you repent of your sins and put your faith in Jesus, you are born again and adopted into God's family. God confirms your adoption by writing your name in His book. You will spend eternity with Him after you die. Jesus sent His seventy disciples out in pairs to share the Gospel. They returned and gave a magnificent report of how the Holy Spirit worked through them. But instead of rejoicing with them, Jesus directs their attention to what really matters, saying in Luke 10:20, *"Rejoice that your names are written in heaven."* Jesus stresses again the importance of our names being recorded in heaven. God includes your name in the story He will tell for all eternity!

Pray for People by Name

You don't know the name of *strangers*, but you always know the names of the people you care about. That's why we must get to know people's names and pray for them by name, like the neighbor who lives three houses down. You wave at him whenever he drives by your home in his red Ford truck.

You might pray for him occasionally, but you won't pray for him with any consistency or passion until you get to know his name. But once you know his name, he is no longer a stranger.

When you pray for your loved ones, you pray for them by name because they matter to you. In the same way, every person matters to God. He knows their stories, pain, fears, doubts, and dreams. And He wants them to matter to us enough to pray for them by name.

I'm not suggesting that we shouldn't pray for people groups, cities, nations, and the world. Of course, we should. I've been interceding for people groups for over thirty years. But God also wants us to pray for *individuals*. The God who loves the entire world is always looking for the *one*. Jesus always leaves the ninety-nine who are doing well and chases after the one lost sheep (Luke 15:4-6).

When you pray for people, it's nearly impossible not to care about them. Every time you lift their names to the Father in prayer, God puts more of His love in your heart for them.

Have you ever watched *The Chosen* TV series? If you haven't, I highly recommend it. My favorite scene in the series is the encounter between Jesus and a demon-possessed prostitute named Lilith. As Jesus approaches her, she is frightened and runs out of the tavern.[33]

Jesus follows her outside, and as she runs, He calls after her not by the name everyone else knew but by her birth name: "Mary! Mary of Magdala."

"Who are you?" she says, freezing in her tracks. Shock washes over her face as she turns around.

"How do you know my name?"

Jesus responds, "I, says the Lord who created you. And He who formed you. Fear not, for I have redeemed you. I have called you by name. You are mine."

Her clients called her by her professional name, *Lilith*. But Jesus knew her real name, *Mary*. She felt loved, seen, and valuable in that instant, and Jesus gave her a new identity. No longer was she Lilith, the prostitute, but Mary, daughter of God. Just like Mary Magdalene, Jesus knows *every* sinner's name. He sees past all their sins and mistakes. Nothing they have done can change how Jesus feels about them—He loves them and calls them by name. And Jesus wants us to pray for them by name.

Pray for Five

There are over two billion Catholics, Protestants, and Evangelicals in the world today. If every Christ-follower committed to praying for five people daily, simple math shows us that we could pray for everyone. Obviously, it will be more difficult in countries with a low percentage of Christians, but with God, all things are possible.

This strategy is simple, doable, and scalable. Nearly every child, teenager, and adult knows five people they can pray for and share Jesus with—five friends, neighbors, family members, classmates, teammates, and co-workers.

Is praying for five people the magic formula for bringing billions to Jesus? Of course not! It's merely one strategy God is blessing. We promote praying for five because it is a doable number for every believer. But you can pray for three, five, or ten—however the Lord leads you.

In 2022, my dear friend, Eric Watt, the President of Run Ministries, mobilized 43 million house church believers worldwide to each pray for ten people by name. Because many of these believers live where Christianity is nearly inexistent, Eric asked them to adopt a larger number of people in prayer and evangelism. Their efforts resulted in 430 million people being prayed for by name last year.

A few years ago, Mercy and I wanted to test this Pray For 5 strategy with our kids to see if it worked at home before we exported it to the world. We asked our eleven-year-old daughter, Lauren, if she would pray for five of her friends.

Lauren said, "No, Dad."

My heart sank.

CHAPTER 1

But then I saw a twinkle in Lauren's eye.

"I want to pray for seven friends, Dad!" she exclaimed.

Bam! I love her overachiever spirit!

Lauren began praying for them every day. And after a few weeks of praying for them, she said, "Dad, can I have my friends over for a Bible study for a few weeks?"

Mercy and Lauren hosted seven of her friends at our house for an eight-week Bible study. On the eighth Friday, Lauren shared her testimony of becoming a follower of Christ. In our living room, five of her friends accepted Jesus Christ as their Savior. So, yes, this simple strategy works—even with pre-teens and teens!

Evangelism starts with prayer, but it doesn't end there. Real prayer, birthed by the Spirit, always moves us to mission. Prayer is not the end game. The end game is to share the Gospel with people and then disciple them after they surrender their lives to Christ. Once you start praying for people, the Holy Spirit moves you to share Jesus with them.

I know you are busy and maxed out; I get it—I am, too. But could you take five minutes a day and pray for five people far from God? I'm not asking for five *hours*—just five *minutes*. What do you say? Could you spare five minutes daily to impact someone's eternity?

> Evangelism starts with prayer, but it doesn't end there. Real prayer, birthed by the Spirit, always moves us to mission.

Chapter 1: Takeaways

 KEY POINTS:

- Names matter to God because people matter to God.
- You don't know the names of *strangers,* but you always know the names of people you care about.
- Since God knows every person by name, He wants us to get to know people by name and pray for them.
- There are 8 billion people in the world today. If every Christ-follower committed to praying for five people daily, we could pray for everyone.
- Prayer is only the beginning. The goal is to go from praying to sharing Jesus and discipling people.

 MEMORY VERSE:

Isaiah 43:1: *"Fear not, for I have redeemed you; I have called you by name, you are mine."*

 A PRAYER:

Thank You, Jesus, for calling me by name and engraving my name on the palm of Your hand. Your love for me is amazing. Help me to remember that You love each person in the world as much as You love me. Lord, show me the five people in my circle of influence You want me to pray for by name. As I pray, give me Your heart for them and give me opportunities to share Your love and Your Word with them.

SELF-REFLECTION QUESTIONS:

1. What emotions came up when you read about God calling you by name and writing your name on the palm of His hand? Take a minute or two to meditate on this, and ask God to show you how precious you truly are to Him.

2. Since God loves each human being as much as He loves you, how do you think He wants you to relate to them?

3. Think of a person you see often but you do not know his or her name. Now think of a person whose name you know. Is there a difference in the way you relate to them or think about them?

4. There are 8 billion people living on Earth today, and yet our challenge is for you to pray for five of them who do not know Jesus yet. Is that doable for you? What measures could you take to faithfully pray for those five people on a daily basis?

 CALL TO ACTION:

On the B. L. E. S. S. card on page 155, write out the five names of people in your circle of influence who you are committing to pray for by name on a daily basis. Place that page on your fridge, in your Bible, or wherever it can remind you to pray for them daily.

Or download the *Pray For All* App and sign up to pray for your five friends there. Visit the app for daily inspiration to pray for and bless your friends.

Myra

Huaijin

Theng Shuen

gitte

LOVE LIKE JESUS

"There isn't time, so brief is life, for bickerings, apologies, heartburnings, callings to account. There is only time for loving, and but an instant, so to speak, for that."[34]

— Mark Twain

So now that I began to understand the importance of praying for each person on Earth by name, I knew I had to find a way not only to do that myself, but also to help others do the same. But how? If I followed Jesus' guidance, the answer, I knew, was easy.

Do everything in love. Love like Jesus.

Our job is to love people so well that their hearts open to the Gospel. We can't pry people's hearts with sermons, scare them open with threats, or shame them; we can only love them. Love is the key to winning people's hearts and leading them to Jesus.

> **Our job is to love people so well that their hearts open to the Gospel.**

In his novel, *Snow Falling on Cedars*, David Guterson summarized the meaning of life in six sentences: "None of those other things makes a difference. Love is the strongest thing in the world, you know. Nothing can touch it. Nothing comes close. If we love each other, we're safe from it all. Love is the biggest thing there is."[35]

When Jesus was asked what the two greatest commands are, He replied in Matthew 22:37-40: *"'Love God with all your heart and with all your soul and with all your mind. This is the first and greatest commandment. And the second is like it: 'Love your neighbor as yourself.' All the Law and the Prophets hang on these two commandments."* The Bible contains over 750,000 words, and Jesus summarized all of them in one word—LOVE.

God's plan for evangelism is simple: Love everyone you come in contact with, whether lifelong friends or strangers, so well that their hearts open to Jesus. Always lead with *love*.

B.L.E.S.S.
A Lifestyle of Relational Evangelism

The key to effective evangelism is building authentic relationships that are based on love. That is why we have adopted the B.L.E.S.S. lifestyle as our primary evangelism strategy. It is a relational framework for sharing the Gospel with people far from God. B.L.E.S.S. stands for:

B. Begin with prayer
L. Listen to them
E. Eat with them
S. Serve them
S. Share Jesus

20

Jesus said in Matthew 11:19, *"The Son of Man, on the other hand, feasts and drinks, and you say, 'He's a glutton and a drunkard, and a friend of tax collectors and other sinners!' But wisdom is shown to be right by its results."*

The worst insult the religious leaders could think of hurling at Jesus was, "You're a friend of sinners!" But Jesus wore that title like a badge of honor. He said that wisdom is proved right by its results. His approach to reaching sinners—loving them on the front end—was proven correct by the outstanding results He had.

I love the B.L.E.S.S. model of relational evangelism because it is based on love and friendship. Everyone wants to be loved and blessed regardless of their religion or background. People don't want to be *evangelized*, but they want to be *loved*. If we lead with love and bless people, we can gently and relationally lead them to Christ.

My dear friends, Dave and Jon Ferguson, wrote a brilliant book on the B.L.E.S.S. strategy entitled, *B.L.E.S.S.—5 Everyday Ways to Love Your Neighbor and Change the World.* I highly recommend it to every believer and leader. They explain and live this model better than anyone I know:

"The B.L.E.S.S. practices were created as a simple tool to help you bring the love of God to others. Your motivation is to help them know Jesus and experience eternal life, but people are often surprised to find that these practices make their own lives better too! You will discover that a life of praying, listening, sharing meals, serving, and telling stories is the richest life possible. The everyday rhythm of these five practices will not only change others and change you but also begin to change your whole neighborhood. Those who commit to living out these practices will see the culture around them slowly shift from being just a group of people living in close proximity to each other to a neighborhood of people living in genuine community."[36]

In the following chapters, we will discuss the five practices and habits of the B.L.E.S.S. lifestyle in more detail.

This is our big *holy* audacious goal: we encourage every believer in the world to **pray daily for five people by name and share Jesus with them using the B.L.E.S.S. lifestyle.**

This is more than a strategy or a campaign—it's a lifestyle of praying for people, listening to their hurts, pains, and fears, eating with them, serving them, and sharing Jesus with them. You only have one life to live here on Earth. Why not make it count for eternity by taking as many people with you to heaven as possible.

I knew this method worked as I had, over my years in evangelism, saw its effects and impact dozens of times. It made me think of a time when I met a new friend, Mazz, and was able to show him the beauty of a life with Jesus.

* * *

The smell of ground coffee beans greeted me as I entered a local coffee shop in Albuquerque, New Mexico. I was here to meet my new friend, Mazz. We ordered our drinks, sat down, and chatted briefly. After I broke the ice, I went deeper.

"Mazz, I'd love to hear your story," I said.

He broke eye contact with me and played with the straw in his drink. "Trust me, P.B. You don't want to hear my story. It's a bad story."

At some point during our conversation, Mazz had begun calling me P.B. instead of Pastor Brian, and I decided it was my new favorite nickname. I leaned forward, making my body language match my words.

"No, Mazz. I really want to hear your story. Nobody's perfect. We've all made mistakes, including me."

"Yeah, but not everyone has made mistakes as bad as me. I recently got out of prison. There is nothing good about my story."

"That's okay. My brother John is in prison right now. I won't judge you."

Mazz finally lifted his head and locked eyes with mine, trying to determine if I meant what I said. After a few seconds, he said, "Okay. What do you want to know?"

"I can tell you were born at some point," I said with a smile. "Start there and catch me up to now."

Mazz grinned.

"Well, I had a rough childhood. I got involved with drugs when I was nine years old. I became a violent person and hurt many people. Eventually, I was sentenced to prison." He shrugged. "There's not much else to say."

I held his gaze compassionately.

"Thank you for sharing that, Mazz. That was extremely brave of you. You made some poor decisions along the way, but those decisions don't have to define you. I would love to be your friend and help you build a new life."

Mazz seemed to consider my words for a minute.

"I became a Muslim in prison, and I hate Christians. So, it won't work if you try to convert me."

"I'm not trying to convert you. I genuinely want to be your friend," I said, and I truly meant it.

"What do you say? Will you give me a chance?" I extended my hand in friendship.

Mazz still wasn't convinced.

"I don't believe you. All you Christians are the same. You just want to convert me."

"Mazz, I would love nothing better than for you to believe as I do, but we won't even discuss my faith if you don't want to. If for some reason down the road you have questions about what I believe, then I will do my best to answer them. In the meantime, all I ask is for a chance to discuss the Prophet Isa after I have earned your trust."

Mazz looked at my still-outstretched hand.

"Alright, deal," Mazz said as he took my hand.

Mazz and I began hanging out and sharing a meal at least once a month. Restaurants, coffee shops, my house, you name it. We played basketball once, and Mazz destroyed me, twenty-one to two. From then on, I suggested we watch basketball on TV instead. I continued praying for Mazz daily, listening to him, eating with him, and building our friendship.

And while the Holy Spirit was working on Mazz, He was also working on me. I didn't realize how much bias I had toward Muslims that I needed to repent of.

We often consider prayer a passive task, but prayer is anything but passive. I discovered that the more I prayed for Mazz, the more I cared for him, and the more I cared for him, the more I wanted to help him. That's how prayer works. Prayer launches us into the battle for people's souls. God wants to use prayer to set a fire in your heart and send you to people and places you never imagined.

One day, Mazz and I were eating at Chick-fil-A, and I asked him how I could serve him. Mazz said he needed a job, so I helped him find one. When befriending people, don't just tell people that God loves them; show them love with your actions. Either meet their needs or connect them to someone who can.

After sixteen months of building my friendship with Mazz, I felt I had finally earned his trust enough to share my faith. We agreed to meet at Starbucks on the corner of Coors and Montaño.

As I turned into the parking lot, I could feel the adrenaline rush. I was overjoyed, but I was also worried about damaging our friendship. Mazz didn't trust many people, and that he trusted me was not something I took for granted.

At Starbucks, Mazz and I briefly discussed how his new job was going. Then I asked him, "Mazz, do you remember what I asked you the first time we met for coffee?"

He shook his head, indicating he didn't.

"I asked you if I could share with you about the Prophet Isa once I earned your trust. Do you trust me?"

"Yeah."

"No, I mean for real. Do you trust me?"

Mazz paused momentarily and then said, "With all my heart, P.B. You're the only white person I have ever trusted."

Those words echoed in my heart. I realized how much it meant for Mazz to say that.

"Thank you! And I trust you, Mazz."

I took a deep breath and activated my courage.

"Mazz, I've read the Quran three times, and it talks a lot about the Prophet Isa. Did you know your holy book says that Isa is the Messiah?"

"Yes."

"Well, guess what? My holy book says the same thing. Isn't that amazing?"

"Um, I guess so."

"Did you know the Quran teaches Isa was born of a virgin and performed miracles?"

Mazz nodded.

"And did you know your holy book says that Isa is coming back to the Earth in the last days to judge the wicked and reward the righteous?"

"Sure."

"Mazz, as your holy book says, Isa is the Messiah, and He will return to Earth in the last days. So is there any chance Isa could be a false prophet?"

"Of course not!" Mazz said emphatically.

"Is there any way Isa was a lunatic and a liar?"

Mazz shook his head. "Absolutely not!"

"Well, let me share with you one more thing about Isa. It's not in your holy book, but it's in mine."

Mazz nodded for me to proceed.

"You call Him Isa in Arabic, but we call Him .
English. And Jesus said He is the way, the truth, and the life
and that He is the only way to the Father. He came to Earth
and died on the cross for your sins and my sins. Jesus loves
you, Mazz. And He wants to adopt you into His family and
give you a life worth living."

As I explained the Good News of Jesus Christ, tears
formed in Mazz's eyes. Mazz tried to speak, then clenched
his jaw against the tidal wave of emotions swelling inside
him.

"What do I need to do?" he finally said.

"It's simple but powerful. The Bible says if you confess
with your mouth that Jesus is Lord and believe in your heart
that God raised Him from the dead, you will be saved. Do
you believe God raised Jesus from the dead? And do you
confess Him as the Lord of your life?"

"Yes," Mazz said, his voice cracking.

After sixteen months of love, prayer, shared meals, and
friendship, Jesus saved my Muslim friend Mazz and adopted
him into His family. An angel wrote Mazz's name in the
Book of Life in heaven that day. We were both overcome
with emotion.

That experience with Mazz taught me that people need
to experience love and grace before they will believe in our
truth. The Bible says in John 1:14, *"The Word became flesh
and made his dwelling among us. We have seen his glory, the
glory of the one and only Son, who came from the Father, full
of grace and truth."*

Jesus was full of *grace* and *truth*. Notice that grace comes before truth. We often try to force people to believe our truth before we allow them to experience God's grace. And that doesn't work because that is not God's order.

> **Jesus was full of grace and truth. Notice that grace comes before truth.**

When the religious leaders in Jesus' day caught a woman in the act of adultery, they dragged her into the streets and threw her on the ground, demanding capital punishment. How did Jesus respond? He showed her grace and protected her from being stoned. Then Jesus told her, "Go and sin no more" (John 8:11). *Grace* first, then *truth*. That's the Jesus way.

Even though I didn't know the B.L.E.S.S. acronym when I led Mazz to Christ, all the B.L.E.S.S. practices were part of my journey with him. And not only with Mazz, but virtually everyone I have led to Christ and discipled has involved these five practices: *praying, listening, eating, serving*, and *sharing*.

By NAME

 **pray for all**

Pray For All is a global initiative to pray for every person in the world by name and share Jesus with them. Our B.L.E.S.S. strategy is not a short-term campaign but a lifestyle.

B.L.E.S.S. – A *Lifestyle* of relational evangelism

B. BEGIN WITH PRAYER

Who you pray for, you care for. When you pray for people by name, God gives you His love for them and opens their hearts to the Gospel. *"I have called you by name" (Isaiah 43:1).*

 PRAY for 5   TAKE 5 MINUTES A DAY TO **PRAY FOR 5** PEOPLE WHO NEED JESUS

L. LISTEN TO THEM

Relationships are built one conversation at a time. Listen to people with empathy and get to know their story, fears, needs, and doubts. *"Everyone should be quick to listen, slow to speak and slow to become angry" (James 1:19).*

E. EAT WITH THEM

Jesus spent a lot of His time eating with people far from God. Eating with people builds friendship and trust. *"While Jesus was having dinner at Matthew's house, many sinners came and ate with him" (Matthew 9:10).*

S. SERVE THEM

Jesus modeled that the best way to reach people is to serve them in practical ways and meet their needs. *"The Son of Man did not come to be served, but to serve, and to give his life as a ransom for many" (Matthew 20:28).*

S. SHARE JESUS WITH THEM

When Paul shared the Gospel in Acts 22, he shared the three parts of his story. Share your life before Jesus, how you met Jesus, and your life since you met Jesus. And then introduce them to God's story, the Gospel.

prayforall.com
Scan the QR Code
to sign up
to pray for 5

Chapter 2: Takeaways

 KEY POINTS:

- Love is the key to winning people's hearts and leading them to Jesus.
- God's plan for evangelism is simple: Love everyone you come in contact with, whether lifelong friends or strangers, so well that their hearts open to Jesus.
- People need to experience love and grace before they will believe in our truth.
- People don't want to be *evangelized,* but they want to be *loved.* If we lead with love and bless people, we can gently and relationally lead them to Christ.
- B.L.E.S.S. is a lifestyle and relational framework for sharing the Gospel with people far from God:

    B. Begin with prayer
    L. Listen to them
    E. Eat with them
    S. Serve them
    S. Share Jesus

 MEMORY VERSE:

Matthew 22:37-40: *"'Love God with all your heart and with all your soul and with all your mind.' This is the first and greatest commandment. And the second is like it: 'Love your neighbor as yourself.' All the Law and the Prophets hang on these two commandments."*

A PRAYER:

Lord, help me to love people the way You love them. Help me to love them so well that their hearts open to the Gospel. Use me as a vessel of Your love.

 SELF-REFLECTION QUESTIONS:

1. Think back to when you came to faith. Who shared the Gospel with you, and how did they help you open your heart to Jesus?

2. If you did not come to faith because of the witness and kindness of someone you knew, do you think that if someone would have B.L.E.S.S.-ed you the way Brian wrote about, it would have made a difference in you coming to Jesus sooner or more fully? Why or why not?

3. How do you currently share your faith with others? How effective is your strategy in winning people to Jesus? How do you think incorporating B.L.E.S.S. into your evangelism strategy can help bring people to Jesus?

 CALL TO ACTION:

Now that you know the five names of the people you are praying for on a daily basis, do a quick inventory of how you have B.L.E.S.S.-ed each of the five people so far. Then write down any opportunities you see to be a B.L.E.S.S.-ing to them.

CHAPTER 3
BEGIN WITH PRAYER

"Prayer is crucial in evangelism: Only God can change the heart of someone who is in rebellion against Him. No matter how logical our arguments or how fervent our appeals, our words will accomplish nothing unless God's Spirit prepares the way."[37]

— **Billy Graham**

"Alarid, come back in here! I need to talk to you."

The voice of my college professor, Lisa, rang out from behind me and chased me down as I tried to escape the classroom. I froze in place with my backpack dangling from one shoulder.

"Why are you running off so fast?" Lisa asked as my classmates continued to pick up their books and shuffle past me out the door.

"Uh, I was in a hurry to return to work," I stammered, nerves on edge.

"Stick around for a few minutes. We need to talk."

All my nerves tensed as I walked back into the slowly emptying room. The minutes seemed to crawl by in slow motion for what seemed like the next twelve years, but in reality, it was only a minute.

Let me rewind for forty-five minutes.

It was the first day of my undergraduate interpersonal communication class. My professor, Lisa, began the lecture with a simple communication assignment: Stand up and tell us your name, what you do for a living, your passion, and describe yourself in one word.

I thought, *This is a good chance to share Jesus and make some new friends.* I was fired up when my turn rolled around.

"Hi, my name is Brian Alarid," I said confidently. "I'm a pastor. My passion is sharing the love of Jesus Christ with people. And I would describe myself in one word as passionate."

Crickets. No one clapped in approval of my boldness. No one even smiled at me to hint that they were believers, too.

After several seconds of awkward silence, I sat down and wanted to disappear. Not exactly how I wanted to kick-start my new semester. I already had a bachelor's degree, but one of the main reasons I enrolled in this class was to make new friends and lead them to Christ. So much for that!

I endured the rest of Lisa's lecture, and as soon as class was dismissed, I made a beeline for the exit. That's when Lisa called out my name and asked to talk with me.

"So, Mr. Alarid, what's your deal?"

"What do you mean?" I asked.

"I want to clarify that I don't tolerate any religious intolerance in my class."

"Excuse me?" I whimpered.

Lisa didn't miss a beat.

"If you try to push your religion on everyone without their consent, I will drop you from my class right now. Are we clear?"

"Crystal," I replied.

My already damaged hope for reaching people for Christ cracked further. Instead of winning people to Jesus, I was repelling them—and it was only the first day of class!

"I'm sorry, Lisa. I didn't mean to offend anyone. I'm not a religious person. In fact, I hate religion, but I really love Jesus. Sometimes my passion for Jesus just takes over. But I promise you; it won't happen again."

As I turned to walk out, Lisa spoke up.

"I used to be a Christian."

I stopped myself mid-stride.

"But now I'm an atheist," Lisa continued. "And if a god does exist, she is definitely a woman."

Wow! That turned fast.

"Ahem," I said. "Well, have a great day, Lisa. See you Thursday."

But Lisa wasn't done. Not even close.

"Doesn't that offend you, Brian?"

I stopped myself for a second time.

"Uh, no, not really. Let's just agree to disagree, okay?"

"Why aren't you upset?" Lisa pushed.

"You have a right to your own beliefs like everyone else. They don't bother me. Jesus doesn't have an identity crisis in heaven. Whether you believe He doesn't exist or is a woman doesn't change how He feels about you. Jesus loves you, died for you, and has a great plan for your life."

Lisa rolled her eyes and folded her arms in disgust.

"Okay, we're done. I can't believe this. You can leave now!"

Now, who's being intolerant? I thought to myself.

CHAPTER 3

After that painfully awkward encounter, I called Mercy on the way back to the office. Mercy tried to console me, but it would take more than words to comfort me—I needed ice cream, gallons of ice cream. As I ate my second pint of *Cherry Garcia*, I scolded myself sarcastically, *You put on a real evangelism clinic today. Great job, Brian!*

Before we fell asleep that night, Mercy challenged me.

"Brian, let's pray for Lisa."

After Lisa chewed me out, praying for her wasn't at the top of my to-do list. But Mercy's words touched my heart, and I knew she was right.

I nodded. "Okay. Let's do it."

Against my anger and self-vindication, I joined hands with Mercy.

"You got this," Mercy said with a smile.

"Jesus, thank you for Lisa," I prayed. "She's smart, articulate, and passionate. I know You love her so much. She obviously has something negative in her past that affects how she sees You. I pray You will heal her heart and bring her back to You."

Two days later, I attended class again and tried to fit in. *Don't make any waves, Brian.*

I tried to sneak out quickly after class—no such luck.

"Hey, Brian! Can you stick around for a minute?" Lisa shouted at me as I was halfway through the exit door.

Are we really going to do this again? I thought.

"Sure," I said reluctantly. As I waited for the other students to exit the room, I braced myself for the onslaught of angry words I was sure were coming.

36

"Thanks for staying, Brian. Do you want to walk me to the cafeteria and have coffee before my next class?"

"Uh, I mean…" I stuttered.

"I don't mean to impose on you, Brian. If you're busy, we can connect another day."

"No, it's fine. I need to return to work soon, but I can talk for a bit."

What is going on?

Lisa paid for our drinks, and we sat down outside.

"Thanks for having coffee with me, Brian. I want to follow up on our conversation the other day. I'm sorry if I came across as abrasive. I didn't mean to insult you."

"No, don't worry about it. It's fine."

"I grew up as a Methodist but switched to the Catholic church in college. But I got hurt and gave up on faith altogether. Can I ask you a few questions?"

"Sure. I've been hurt by religion, too, so I understand your reluctance."

"Thanks for saying that. There's something different about you…you're not like other Christians I've met."

"The movement Jesus built was based on faith, hope, and love, but much of Christianity has become judgmental and polarizing. And I don't identify with that at all."

"What do you mean?" she asked.

"Well, the Bible says that God is love. And whoever lives in love lives in God. And God lives in them. The defining feature of what it means to be a follower of Jesus is love."

Lisa leaned in. I could tell she was genuinely interested. So I continued.

"Many Christians condemn anyone who doesn't think like them. But that's not the way Jesus modeled it. I want to live in love like Jesus."

Our impromptu coffee break continued until Lisa's next class started, and a friendship was born. Over the following months, we met for coffee several more times. Mercy and I took Lisa out to lunch, and Lisa invited us over to her home for Easter. The whole time, I continued to pray for her by name every day.

After the last class of the semester, Lisa invited Mercy and me to join her for lunch at Olive Garden.

"Brian, when you first joined my class, I didn't like you," Lisa said, laughing.

"Oh, I didn't notice!" I chuckled.

"But you've surprised me. You're one of the nicest, most genuine people I've ever met."

"Thanks, Lisa. I'm happy we became friends. And honestly, I loved your class! Well, except for maybe that first day," I said jokingly, and we all laughed again.

Lisa said, "You know what's funny? I gave up on God many years ago. But now you've got me asking questions again."

"Lisa, Jesus loves you just as you are," I replied. "Jesus knows you have been hurt. He knows you have doubts and questions and fears. And He loves you through all of them. If you give Jesus a chance, He will give you a new life."

I explained the Gospel to Lisa, and she opened her heart to Jesus over a bowl of fettuccine alfredo. I'm telling you, there must have been *a heavy anointing* on that pasta!

Granted, Lisa and I had many encounters before that day. Her change of heart and mind didn't happen overnight. What difference did it make that I prayed for Lisa that whole time? Couldn't I have skipped that part and shared the Gospel with her? Sure, but doing so would have been like planting good seeds in dry, hardened soil.

The Bible describes prayer as a tool that softens people's hearts to receive the Gospel, much like a plow tills the ground for the seed to take root. Jesus said in John 6:44, *"No one can come to me unless the Father who sent me draws them."* When we pray for people, the Father draws them to His Son. That's what happened with Lisa.

Begin with Prayer

The first habit in the B.L.E.S.S. lifestyle is to *begin with prayer*. Evangelism begins and ends with prayer.

In his sermon entitled, *Soul Winning*, Charles Spurgeon said, "The soul-winner must be a master of the art of prayer. You cannot bring souls to God if you go not to God yourself. You must get up your battle-axe and your weapons of war, from the armory of sacred communion with Christ.

"If you are much alone with Jesus, you will catch his Spirit; you will be fired with the flame that burned in his breast and consumed his life. You will weep with the tears that fell upon Jerusalem when he saw it perishing." [38]

As in any relationship, the closer you become, the more aware you are of that person's passions and burdens. The closer we grow to God, the more we realize He wants to save the people around us. As you pray, God will give you a burden to partner with Him in that quest.

God loves partnering with people. He could have liberated the Israelites from Egypt with a single thought, but He sent Moses. God could have killed Goliath with a word from His mouth, but He sent David. He could have preserved the Jews in Persia by single-handedly eliminating their enemies, but He worked through Esther.

And while our role in saving mankind may not become a motion picture as theirs did, God still invites men and women like you into this epic battle for souls. We don't fight with swords or machine guns. Prayer, the weapon God has given us, defies logic and confounds the enemy. Prayer is a two-way conversation between God and us about the people He loves.

The prophet said in Isaiah 6:8: *"Then I heard the voice of the Lord saying, 'Whom shall I send? And who will go for us?' And I said, 'Here am I. Send me!'"* Just like Isaiah, God is inviting you and me to partner with Him. The Father is asking, "Whom shall I send?"

"Whom shall I send to feed that homeless man?"

"Whom shall I send to buy groceries for that single mom?"

"Whom shall I send to share My love with the high schooler in the back of the room with cuts on her arm?"

"Whom shall I send to serve that angry co-worker?"

"Whom shall I send to witness to that hell-bent, cocaine-snorting, obnoxious neighbor?"

We have a choice. We can answer the call like the Prophet Isaiah did or ignore God. But if we answer and join God on the battlefield for souls, He will do miracles beyond our wildest dreams.

1 John 5:14-15 tells us, *"This is the confidence we have in approaching God: that if we ask anything according to his will, he hears us. And if we know that he hears us—whatever we ask—we know that we have what we asked of him."* We know it is God's will to save the people around us. When we pray, He activates His power on our behalf and theirs.

At its core, prayer is both relational and missional. God created us to commune and fellowship with Him, and as we commune with Him, He gives us His burden to reach people far from Him. Biblical, Spirit-empowered prayer is not about experiencing the goosebumps of being in God's presence, but about empowering us for mission. Pray, get charged up in God's presence, and then go share God's love with people far from Him.

Daily Prayer for Your Five

Here is a prayer that you can pray every day for your five. I encourage you to memorize it and pray it daily:

God, I thank You for Your rescuing heart that longs to save my friends, family, and neighbors (1 Tim. 2:4). And for intentionally placing me here to join You in that labor (Acts 17:26). I lift them up before Your gracious throne (1 Tim.

2:1). You created them, You love them, and You want to rule in their home (Ezek. 37:27).

Save them, Lord. Reveal Yourself. Help them see You (Mt. 11:27). Soften their hearts to Your Word. For Jesus, make them thirsty (Ezek. 36:26). Set up appointments between us so that I may share Your Gospel's freedom (Acts 8:26-27). Use me in their lives to be salt and light for Your glory and Your kingdom (Mt. 5:13-14).

I know what you are thinking: Can praying for five people *really* make a difference? Let me share a few examples that will inspire and encourage you.

George Müller was a Christian evangelist who cared for over 10,000 orphans and established 117 schools in his lifetime. He shared this incredible story about praying for five people in his journal.

"In November 1844, I began to pray for the conversion of five individuals. I prayed every day without one single intermission, whether sick or in health, on the land or on the sea, and whatever the pressure of my engagements might be. Eighteen months elapsed before the first of the five was converted. I thanked God, and prayed on for the others.

"Five years elapsed, and then the second one was converted. I thanked God for the second, and prayed on for the other three. Day by day I continued to pray for them and six years more passed before the third was converted. I thanked God for the three, and went on praying for the other two. These two remain unconverted.

"…[I have] been praying day by day for nearly thirty-six years for the conversion of these two individuals, and yet they remain unconverted; for next November it will be thirty-six years since I began to pray for their conversion. But I hope in God, I pray on, and look yet for the answer."[39]

One of the two men was saved before Müller died in 1898, and the other surrendered his life to Christ afterward. He prayed for his five friends for over *fifty-four* years! Talk about perseverance in prayer!

I'm not asking you to pray for five people for a few weeks or months. I'm encouraging you to adopt them in prayer and pray for them as long as it takes until they accept Jesus Christ as their Lord and Savior, even if it takes fifty-four years.

And once they accept Jesus as their Savior, continue praying for them and encourage them to adopt five people in prayer. Your prayers can transform their lives and the lives they will touch.

John Balasing shared this story with us through our *Pray For All* app: "After praying for a month, one of my five, Mr. Rajinder, gave up the habit of taking liquor and accepted the Lord Jesus as his Savior. Praise God!"

Luis Alvarado, a pastor in Guatemala, shared this testimony at our conference in September 2022: "Why had it not occurred to any of us in Guatemala to pray for five? Someone from afar had to come to our country to teach us this simple concept! And we thank God for that because we took it to heart and prayed. To our surprise, many church members accepted the challenge and listed people for whom they wanted to pray.

"As the pastor, I kept the complete list of the 250 names we were praying for as a church, and I quickly realized that many were the names of the gang members in our sector. People in our area realized we were praying for the gang members and their families. Shortly thereafter, the families of well-known gang members in prison began attending our church.

"About a month ago, the head of a gang asked my son to come to his house. I was worried and didn't know why he wanted to see my son. We told his guys my son was not home, so they left. A few minutes later, the messengers came again, asking me to go with them to meet with their boss.

"When I arrived, the head of the gang was weeping under God's conviction. He had been extorting people out of their money, and he had recently found out that they were members of our church. He had asked me to come so he could ask for my forgiveness and promise never to do that again to my people.

"Two days ago, relatives of another gang member and the wife of yet another attended our church. For a moment, I worried about the safety of our church, but my daughter wisely told me, 'Dad, don't worry. Let's help them, show them love and allow God to work in their lives.'

"We are witnessing incredible results in our community as we pray for people far from God. I encourage every pastor to engage their church in praying for five people for five minutes a day. It really works!"

My wife, Mercy, prayed by name every day for three months for a lady who works for us. She saw her daily, so it wasn't hard for her to find opportunities to listen to her, share meals with her, and serve her.

Although there has been ample time to form a close-knit bond, this lady has kept her distance and set firm boundaries in how she relates to us. Mercy prayed for her every day, no matter how distant this person seemed.

Recently, she became ill and had to take time off work. Overnight, she had lost most of her vision in one eye, and her other eye was blurry. She called Mercy to tell her the news and asked her to pray. Mercy committed to praying for her healing daily.

As Mercy prayed one night, the Lord impressed upon her to keep paying her 75% of what she previously earned, even though she was at home resting. I didn't question it, since it was a word from the Lord. When Mercy shared with this woman that we would continue paying her, she couldn't believe it and thanked her for providing for her and her kids.

Doctors had told her that her vision loss was irreversible. Still, she would text Mercy to thank her for her prayers because her vision was improving daily. She said, "This is a miracle! I shouldn't be improving, but I know it's because you're praying for me." We continued praying for her healing and salvation as a family. Five weeks later, she felt well enough to return to work for a few hours, and as the days went by, she grew stronger and stronger.

A few days ago, Mercy told her she would give her a ride to the bus stop since we had kept her later than expected. The traffic was horrendous that day, but Mercy sensed the delay was a God-ordained opportunity to share Christ with her.

On the ride there, the woman opened her heart. She shared many painful stories from her past and eventually told Mercy she was ready to follow Jesus. Mercy explained the Gospel to her, and she was receptive. They have set up a weekly time to go through a Bible study together.

My daughter, Chloe, is nineteen years old. Like many young people, she loves Instagram and enjoys befriending people on the app who comment on her posts. One night, she responded to a young man who asked questions about her faith. They've had many conversations since then, and Chloe prays for him daily.

He talks to her about his distaste for Christians, who preach grace but are not gracious. His questions are complex and often loaded with anger and resentment. While it does not seem like he is growing closer to trusting Christ, I love what is happening inside Chloe's heart.

Chloe explained it to me like this: "Praying for him has given me compassion for him and other young people who grew up as Jehovah's Witnesses. The god he learned about is not the God I know, and I want to stay in his life long enough for him to meet Jesus.

"He often asks me questions about Christianity I don't know the answers to. So that pushes me to study the Bible for myself to help him. Praying for an unbeliever like him has changed my life."

Pray Consistently

Monica was a devout follower of Christ who lived in present-day Algeria. She was married to a Roman official, Patricius, and they had three children: Augustine, Navigius, and Perpetua. (Very common names!) Augustine was her most intellectually gifted and most difficult child.

When Augustine was seventeen, he left to study philosophy in Carthage, where he began a long-term affair with a mistress, and they had a child out of wedlock. To make matters worse, he joined a religious cult.

Monica prayed for Augustine relentlessly and often begged him to repent. But he ignored all her pleas. You may have found yourself in a similar position with your son, daughter, parents, or friend. And no matter how much you pray for them and reach out to them, they still won't listen!

One day, Monica took a different approach and asked a bishop to speak with her son. He refused because he thought Augustine was too far gone. Monica continued to plead with the bishop with tears streaming down her face.

Finally, overwhelmed by her broken spirit, the bishop threw his hands up and exclaimed: "Go! Leave me alone. As you live, it is impossible that the son of such tears should perish."[40]

After fourteen years, Augustine surrendered his life to Jesus. You may know him as *Saint Augustine*—one of history's most influential Christian leaders. Augustine was running from God as fast as he could, but he couldn't outrun his mother's prayers.

I encourage you to keep praying. Keep fighting for your loved ones. God delights in restoring prodigals. Don't give up on them. Your loved ones may rebel repeatedly, but they can't outrun your prayers. Paul comforts us in Romans 5:20: *"Where sin abounds, grace does much more abound."* Your loved one might be bound by sin, but God's grace is more abundant. His grace trumps sin every time.

Pastor Jack Hayford laid his hands on my mom's stomach when she was eight months pregnant with me and prayed over me. As a teenager, I tried to run away from God, but it didn't work. I couldn't outrun the prayers that had been prayed over me since before I was born. You could say I was *ruined* from birth! Thank you, Mom, for never giving up on me and always praying for me.

I know what it is like to pray for someone who refuses to repent. I prayed for my brother for fifteen years before he turned from his life as a drug dealer and committed his life to Christ. Today, John leads a thriving church and several addiction recovery homes in Springfield, Missouri.

My friend, Evelyn Davison, prayed for over fifty years for her dad to accept Christ, and he finally did. Prayer does not go unanswered. With enough time and consistency, water can penetrate the thickest rock, and prayer can break through the hardest of hearts.

Occasional exercise won't give you the physical results you want. Nothing in your life will produce much fruit unless you do it *consistently*. Best-selling author Anthony Robbins put it this way: "It's not what we do once in a while that shapes our lives. It's what we do consistently."[41] Just as with physical discipline, our prayer life must also be consistent to yield fruit.

Paul prayed *daily* by name for the people he loved. He wrote a letter to his spiritual son in 2 Timothy 1:3: *"Timothy, I thank God for you—the God I serve with a clear conscience, just as my ancestors did. Night and day, I constantly remember you in my prayers."*[42]

Similarly, Paul writes to his friend in Philemon 1:4: *"I always thank my God as I remember you in my prayers."* Paul didn't pray for his loved ones occasionally; he prayed for them constantly *by name*. Consistent prayer produces consistent results.

How to Pray for Unbelievers

I am often asked, "How do I pray for my unsaved friends and family?" I have written five biblical prayers that you can use to pray for people far from God.

1. Father, draw them to Your Son, Jesus (John 6:44). Start by asking God to draw them to Jesus. Unless God draws them, nothing you can say will make a difference. I pray this every day for my unsaved friends.

2. Father, remove their spiritual blindness so they will believe the Gospel (2 Corinthians 4:4; Acts 16:14). People don't believe in Jesus because the devil has blinded them from understanding the truth. So pray that God will remove that spiritual blindness and open their spiritual eyes.

3. Father, give them the gift of repentance to turn from their sins (John 16:8; 2 Timothy 2:25-26). Unless

God gives people the gift of repentance, they can't change. Repentance is both a gift from God and a human response to God's grace. Pray that the Holy Spirit will convict them and bring them to repentance.

4. Father, give me opportunities and boldness to share the Gospel with them (Colossians 4:3-4; Acts 4:29-31). Pray that God will remove every distraction and barrier so they will be receptive to hearing about Christ. You must be bold and seize the opportunity when their hearts are open. The apostles prayed for boldness to share Christ.

5. Father, save them and their whole family (Acts 16:31). Finally, pray that God will save them and their entire family, too. God cares about families, and His grace is sufficient to save *entire* families, like in Acts 16 with the Philippian jailer.

Call to Action

Will you pray for five people by name for at least five minutes daily? Write their names and begin praying for them today. Start with one if you can't think of five people.

Name _Jeff ~ Tim ~ Ken_

Name _Brian @ Diana_

Name _Carrie @ John_

Name _Scotty ~ Tobi_

Name _Julie @ parents_

Chapter 3: Takeaways

 KEY POINTS:

- Evangelism starts and ends with prayer.
- Prayer softens peoples' hearts to receive the Gospel, much like a plow prepares the soil to receive and nurture the seeds being planted.
- At its core, prayer is both relational and missional. God created us to commune and fellowship with Him, and as we commune with Him, He gives us His burden to reach people far from Him.
- Biblical, Spirit-empowered prayer is not about experiencing the goosebumps of being in God's presence, but about empowering us for mission.
- Consistent prayer produces consistent results.

 MEMORY VERSE:

1 John 5:14-15: *"This is the confidence we have in approaching God: that if we ask anything according to his will, he hears us. And if we know that he hears us—whatever we ask—we know that we have what we asked of him."*

 A PRAYER:

Place the names of your five friends in the blank spaces as you pray this prayer daily: God, I thank You for Your rescuing heart that longs to save *Jeff* *Tom*, *Ken*, *Deana*, *Carrie*, and *Julie*

And for intentionally placing me here to join You in that labor. I lift them up before Your gracious throne. You created them, You love them, and You want to rule in their home. Save them, Lord. Reveal Yourself. Help them see You. Soften their hearts to Your Word. For Jesus, make them thirsty. Set up appointments between us so that I may share Your Gospel's freedom. Use me in their lives to be salt and light for Your glory and Your kingdom.

 SELF-REFLECTION QUESTIONS:

1. Why do you think God wants us to talk to Him about the people He already desperately wants to save?
2. Think of an instance when praying fired the flame of evangelism in your heart.
3. What is one important thing you do consistently in your daily life? Why do you do it? What do you think might happen if you prayed as consistently for your five as you do this one important thing?

 CALL TO ACTION:

Fill out the B.L.E.S.S. card (after Chapter 8) with the names of five people far from God you can pray for on a daily basis. Feel free to tear it out of this book and place it somewhere visible (on your refrigerator, in your Bible, etc.) that will remind you to pray for your five on a daily basis. You can also download our *Pray For All* app, and fill out this card digitally. On the app, you will receive reminders, inspiration, and encouragement to help you consistently pray for your five.

CHAPTER 4
LISTEN TO THEM

*"Listening is a magnetic and strange thing, a creative force.
The friends who listen to us are the ones we move toward.
When we are listened to, it creates us, makes us unfold and
expand."*[43]

— **Karl A. Menninger**

In the same classroom where my professor, Lisa, had read me the riot act a few weeks before, she encouraged us to get into groups so we could start to work on a new project.

One particular student caught my attention. Her hijab was a kaleidoscope of colors, making her impossible to miss even in a crowded classroom.

"Hi, my name is Brian! Great to meet you," I said, walking up to her.

"Hello! I'm Nemo."

"Where are you from?" I asked.

"Albuquerque," she said sarcastically. "But I'm from Egypt originally, if that's what you mean."

"That's cool! Would you like to join my group?"

With a smile and a nod, Nemo politely accepted my invitation, as did a few other classmates. After hearing about the assignment, we agreed to meet two days later to work on the project. We met at a busy Starbucks, and after we ordered our drinks and sat at our table, I leaned in.

"So, what's it like in Egypt?" I asked Nemo excitedly. "Is it as beautiful as it looks in the pictures and movies?"

Nemo's face lit up as she told us about Egypt. But as the conversation continued, I could hear a hint of sadness creep into her voice.

"How are you adjusting to life in America?" I prodded.

"Honestly, it's been hard. I miss my family. And sometimes, I get strange looks for the way I dress. It's like some Americans have never seen a Muslim before!"

"I'm so sorry, Nemo. I can only imagine how hard that must be."

After that conversation, I made it a point to sit by her in class, and our conversations before and after class grew deeper and more frequent. I began praying for Nemo by name every day and asked God to lead her to Him through me.

One day, I worked up the nerve to ask Nemo about her Muslim faith and what she heard when she prayed to Allah. I was genuinely curious.

"What do you mean?" she asked, visibly confused. "Allah doesn't talk to me when I pray…Why? Does your God talk to you?"

"Every day. It's my favorite part of prayer. I'd get tired of praying if all I did was listen to myself talk," I said jokingly.

Then, I had an idea that seemed like a God thought. So, I challenged her, "The next time you pray, why don't you ask Allah to speak to you?"

I wasn't sure this was a good idea, but I knew she wasn't open to speaking with Jesus yet. Nemo looked down and seemed to get uncomfortable.

"I don't know about that...I have to go. Have a good weekend."

A few weeks later, Nemo approached me before class. "I tried what you suggested. I asked Allah to talk to me."

"That's cool! Did it work?"

"No, Allah didn't speak to me," she shrugged. "I told you it was a bad idea!"

"I'm sorry, Nemo...But what about this? Mohammed talks a lot about the Prophet Isa in the Quran. Why don't you ask Isa to talk to you the next time you pray?"

"Uh..." she shuffled her feet. "I don't think we're supposed to do that."

"Didn't Mohammed write in the Quran that Isa is the Messiah? So why wouldn't Mohammed want you to pray to the Messiah?"

"I don't know. I just don't know," Nemo sighed, obviously wrestling with stepping outside the box of what she considered appropriate.

I held my breath for what seemed like an eternity, waiting for her to continue.

"Can I ask you something, Brian?" she asked.

"Of course."

"Why are you always so happy? When I first met you, I thought you were fake because nobody can always be that happy. But now that I know you, I know you are real."

"Oh, that's easy, Nemo. Jesus is the reason I'm happy. He loves me and talks to me every day. And Jesus—or Isa, as you would say in Arabic—loves you, too."

"Okay," Nemo said as we both took our seats, and Lisa began her lecture.

On the last day of the semester, Nemo asked if we could talk after class. "I tried what you suggested," she said. "I prayed to the Prophet Isa."

"Really? What happened?" I asked eagerly.

"I didn't hear anything, but I did feel something. This amazing peace I've never felt before came over me."

I smiled as big as the moon.

"I don't know what my parents will say," Nemo continued, "but I want to keep praying to Isa. Thanks for recommending it, Brian. You've been a great friend to me."

Mercy and I left for Europe a week later, and Nemo moved back to Egypt that summer. I never saw her again. Nemo didn't accept Jesus as her Savior that semester, but the Holy Spirit answered my prayer by using me to bring her *closer* to Jesus than she was before I met her.

Twenty years later, I still pray that Nemo will encounter Jesus and surrender to His love. My approach with Nemo was to ask questions, listen to her story, and befriend her. She wasn't open to the Gospel. So I couldn't lead with, "Do you want to become a Christian?"

But I knew if I listened well, asked good questions, and took an interest in her story, I could eventually help open her heart to Jesus. I just had to be patient and plant the seeds of the Gospel in her life little by little.

That strategy didn't just work with Nemo—it works with everyone. People are desperate for someone to listen to them and understand them. Author Ralph Nichols explains, "The most basic of all human needs is the need to understand and be understood. The best way to understand people is to listen to them."[44]

Be Quick to Listen

The second habit in the B.L.E.S.S. lifestyle is to *listen to them*. Listen to the five people you pray for daily. Prayer is only the beginning of this lifestyle. To bless the people we pray for, we must leave our "prayer closet" and engage them in life-giving conversations that make them feel seen and heard. Easier said than done, right?

If you have ever been accused of being a poor listener, welcome to the human race! Most of us have ears and can hear—but we seldom listen. Why? It could be one of several reasons: we might be afraid, self-absorbed, proud, defensive, unteachable, bored, or hurt.

Way too often, we are quick to speak, fast to get angry, and slow to listen. Maybe that is why the Apostle James challenged us to do the opposite: *"Everyone should be quick to listen, slow to speak, and slow to become angry"* (James 1:19). Most people don't listen to understand—they only listen to prepare their rebuttal.

Henri Nouwen shared this insight about listening: "To listen is very hard because it asks of us so much interior stability that we no longer need to prove ourselves by speeches, arguments, statements, or declarations."[45]

So how do we get better at listening? We must come to terms with the fact that listening is both a skill and a gift. Everyone can learn to listen better. It's a skill we should all add to our repertoire of social graces. When you listen, you're attempting to understand people's perspectives while showing them deference and respect.

Alice Duer Miller explains it this way, "Listening... means taking a vigorous, human interest in what is being told us. You can listen like a blank wall or like a splendid auditorium where every sound comes back fuller and richer."[46] While words can certainly communicate love, listening demonstrates it.

Listening is not only a skill but also a gift from God. Proverbs 20:12 says, *"Ears to hear and eyes to see—both are gifts from the Lord."*[47] As you grow in your listening skills, pray that God gives you the ability to listen beyond what is spoken to hear people's hearts and God's heart for them.

Be open for the Holy Spirit to teach you new habits. He will show you how to incline your ear to understand people's stories, pain, fears, and doubts, and build relationships, one conversation at a time.

A Master Class in Listening

When we think of Jesus during His earthly life, we often imagine Him surrounded by crowds while preaching, teaching, or healing as He visited villages and cities in Israel. Jesus was a master communicator and miracle worker, but He was also the master of life-giving conversations.

In John chapter 4, Jesus was on the way to Galilee with His disciples when He felt moved to go through Samaria. While His disciples walked into Samaria to gather supplies, Jesus remained outside the city and rested against the community water well. We read the story in John 4:7-30 from *The Message* translation.

A woman, a Samaritan, came to draw water. Jesus said, "Would you give me a drink of water?" (His disciples had gone to the village to buy food for lunch.)

The Samaritan woman, taken aback, asked, "How come you, a Jew, are asking me, a Samaritan woman, for a drink?" (Jews in those days wouldn't be caught dead talking to Samaritans.)

Jesus answered, "If you knew the generosity of God and who I am, you would be asking *me* for a drink, and I would give you fresh, living water."

The woman said, "Sir, you don't even have a bucket to draw with, and this well is deep. So how are you going to get this 'living water'? Are you a better man than our ancestor Jacob, who dug this well and drank from it, he and his sons and livestock, and passed it down to us?"

Jesus said, "Everyone who drinks this water will get thirsty again and again. Anyone who drinks the water I give will never thirst—not ever. The water I give will be an artesian spring within, gushing fountains of endless life."

The woman said, "Sir, give me this water so I won't ever get thirsty, won't ever have to come back to this well again!"

He said, "Go call your husband and then come back."

"I have no husband," she said.

"That's nicely put: 'I have no husband.' You've had five husbands, and the man you're living with now isn't even your husband. You spoke the truth there, sure enough."

"Oh, so you're a prophet! Well, tell me this: Our ancestors worshiped God at this mountain, but you Jews insist that Jerusalem is the only place for worship, right?"

"Believe me, woman, the time is coming when you Samaritans will worship the Father neither here at this mountain nor there in Jerusalem. You worship guessing in the dark; we Jews worship in the clear light of day. God's way of salvation is made available through the Jews. But the time is coming—it has, in fact, come—when what you're called will not matter and where you go to worship will not matter.

"It's who you are and the way you live that count before God. Your worship must engage your spirit in the pursuit of truth. That's the kind of people the Father is out looking for: those who are simply and honestly *themselves* before him in their worship. God is sheer being itself—Spirit. Those who worship him must do it out of their very being, their spirits, their true selves, in adoration."

The woman said, "I don't know about that. I do know that the Messiah is coming. When he arrives, we'll get the whole story."

"I am he," said Jesus. "You don't have to wait any longer or look any farther."

Just then his disciples came back. They were shocked. They couldn't believe he was talking with that kind of a woman. No one said what they were all thinking, but their faces showed it.

The woman took the hint and left. In her confusion she left her water pot. Back in the village she told the people, "Come see a man who knew all about the things I did, who knows me inside and out. Do you think this could be the Messiah?" And they went out to see for themselves.

Jesus engaged the Samaritan woman in conversation. He listened to her and challenged her thinking. He spoke prophetically into her life and offered her hope. She felt seen, heard, and loved. No other religious leader had ever noticed her, much less listened to her.

Because of her testimony, the whole town came out to meet Jesus. She was a contagious Christian. She hadn't been water baptized, attended church, or completed a new believer's class. Yet she was one of the most effective evangelists in the Bible.

Many people in the Bible got saved because of one conversation, like this woman in John 4. Think about the Ethiopian eunuch in Acts 8, Cornelius in Acts 10, and a businesswoman named Lydia in Acts 16.

Sometimes, you only get one conversation with someone and don't have enough time to go through the whole B.L.E.S.S. lifestyle practices. But if they are ready, and you are, too, you only need one conversation to lead them to Christ.

But all of that starts with a simple conversation. Many people don't know how to have one of those anymore. They weren't taught, and nobody modeled it for them. Television and streaming apps on mobile phones absorb most of our time. Many families sadly no longer engage in conversation. If that describes you, don't feel bad. Everyone can learn to have heartfelt conversations, including you. The first thing we must learn is how to listen well.

Five Qualities of Good Listeners

In their article, *What Great Listeners Actually Do*, Zenger and Folkman share four salient characteristics of outstanding listeners that emerged after studying data from 3,492 participants.[48] I added a fifth quality that I think is critical as well.

1. Good listening is much more than being silent while the other person talks. Zenger and Folkman said, "Good listening was consistently seen as a two-way dialog, rather than a one-way 'speaker versus hearer' interaction."[49]

Besides giving our undivided attention to the speaker, our responses to their comments are the best indicators that we genuinely listen to them. Asking relevant questions throughout the conversation signifies that we are fully engaged. In the exchange between Jesus and the woman at the well, He asked her pertinent and penetrating questions to move the conversation to an intended end.

On another note, communication experts believe 70 to 93% of all communication is non-verbal.[50] Smile, nod your head, lean forward, look them comfortably in their eyes, and affirm them even though you may disagree with what they are saying.

2. Good listening includes interactions that build a person's self-esteem. This is my favorite item because it's the most difficult to do when disagreeing. It's easy to build up someone we agree with, but how do you encourage someone whose ideas, lifestyle, and worldview make your blood boil?

To do this, we have to separate the words from the person. The words we hear are not always accurate, sensible, or acceptable. But the person is always worthy of our patience and respect.

Jesus was so good at this! The woman at the well was an outcast. But Jesus engaged her in a conversation that shocked even the woman.

Listen without letting your biases affect how you respond to people's opinions. Don't tell them their idea is stupid, their plan is ridiculous, or their feelings are invalid. Then go a step farther and let them know you value them, even though you may disagree with them on some points.

3. Good listening is a cooperative conversation. Good listeners are not defensive or competitive. Zenger and Folkman said, "Good listeners may challenge assumptions and disagree, but the person being listened to feels the listener is trying to help, not wanting to win an argument."[51]

Once again, the conversation at the well shows Jesus' mastery of this skill. He refuses to be defensive, leading the woman to hope in a single conversation. What if we approached our conversations with a heart to help instead of needing to be right every time? Listen to understand and help, not to prepare your counterargument.

4. Good listeners tend to make suggestions. Listening well requires us to give feedback. This is where finesse, tact, and hearing from the Holy Spirit play a crucial role in our conversations with unbelievers. Zenger and Folkman debunk the idea of *listening like sponges*, which absorb anything that reaches them.

They say that good listeners are more like trampolines: "They are someone you can bounce ideas off of—and rather than absorbing your ideas and energy, they amplify, energize, and clarify your thinking."[52]

That is what Jesus did for the woman at the well long ago. In a few minutes, she went from deeming Him an enemy to calling Him a prophet and then believing He was the promised Messiah! With a few pointed statements, Jesus became the trampoline that this woman used to jump from hopelessness to eternal life with God.

My dear friend, Tyson Tuttle, the former CEO of Silicon Labs, is a master listener. He often takes notes and summarizes what we discuss at the end. That makes me feel valued. And, because I feel valued, I am more apt to listen to and act on his suggestions and input. He causes me to think differently about life. I can honestly say that I am a different person because of Tyson's influence. (Brothers for life!)

Genuinely listen to the people you are praying for. Chances are you will get windows of opportunity to serve as the trampoline that catapults them to new ways of thinking or living that include God and His Word.

Thinking back to my conversation with Nemo, it had to be the Holy Spirit who prompted me to suggest that Nemo consider talking to the Prophet Isa that day. I never learned that in Bible College, and when I said it, I wondered if I was taking it too far. Still, her response let me know that I had earned enough of her trust to suggest something that broke long-held paradigms for her!

Zenger and Folkman's list ends here, but there is one more quality of skilled listeners that I want to add to theirs because it's just as important as the other four.

5. Good listeners demonstrate empathy. Empathy is the ability to feel how people feel and see things from their perspective. It's the ability to put yourself in their shoes. Most of us are better at *sympathy* (I'm sorry for you) than *empathy* (I understand how you feel). It takes a lot of emotional effort to understand how people feel, see the world through their eyes, and have the humility to validate their feelings.

Empathy says, *I understand how you feel. And if I were in your shoes, I would probably feel the same way.*

In the woman's case, she was a person of ill repute. And while Jesus could not endorse her waywardness, the way He spoke about her misdeeds affected her so much that she even mentioned it when telling others about Him: "Come, see the man who told me everything I ever did! Surely He is the Christ?" She felt not only seen and understood, but valued. That is the epitome of empathy.

CHAPTER 4

I love Peter Drucker's observation: "The most important thing in communication is to hear what isn't being said."[53] Nobody modeled this better than Jesus. He was the master at hearing what people *didn't* say. That's because He loved people so well and listened with empathy that He could hear their hearts.

So here are the five characteristics of a good listener. Which one do you need to improve most to converse effectively with people far from God?

1. Good listening is much more than being silent while the other person talks.
2. Good listening includes interactions that build a person's self-esteem.
3. Good listening is a cooperative conversation.
4. Good listeners tend to make suggestions.
5. Good listeners demonstrate empathy.

How to Spark Good Conversations

Now that you know how to listen well, let me give you some tips to engage others in conversation easily. After all, the key to evangelism is authentic relationships built on love, and relationships are built one conversation at a time.

When I get to know people, I usually start by saying, "I would love to get to know you. Tell me your story." Most people don't know how to tell their stories, so I ask them questions to guide them along.

Here are some questions that can help spark great conversations and build relationships. Commenting on their answers shows you are interested in what they say. Try to maintain eye contact. And whatever you do, avoid politics until you earn their trust.

History and Background:
Where were you born and raised?
Tell me about your family.
Are you married? Do you have children?
Do you have any siblings? Are you close to them?
What are some of your favorite childhood memories?

Employment:
What do you do for a living?
Tell me about your job. Do you enjoy it?
Do you enjoy the people you work with?
What's your dream job?

Social Life:
What are some of your interests or hobbies?
What do you do for fun?
What are your favorite movies, TV shows, and bands?
Tell me about your friends.
What are some things you care about deeply?

Faith:
What is your spiritual background?
Did you grow up with any faith?
If they are Christ-followers, ask them to tell you how they met Jesus.

Has God done anything extraordinary in your life?

Calling, Life, and Purpose:
What is your biggest accomplishment?
Who is your favorite author?
Where do you see yourself in five years?
What are you passionate about?
What gets you fired up?
What do you think are your calling and purpose in life?
If you could do anything, what would it be?
How do you want to be remembered?

Why don't you try practicing some of these questions with someone this week? And as you converse with them, try to listen and make them feel loved and valued. Author Roy T. Bennett gives sage advice on seven effective ways to make others feel important:[54]

1. Use their name.
2. Express sincere gratitude.
3. Do more listening than talking.
4. Talk more about them than about you.
5. Be authentically interested.
6. Be sincere in your praise.
7. Show you care.

Listening to people—to their stories, their hurts, fears, and doubts—without judging them can transform them more than a thousand sermons ever could. People are starving to be heard. Will you listen to them?

Chapter 4: Takeaways

 KEY POINTS:

- Everyone can learn to listen better. It's a skill we should all add to our repertoire of social graces.
- When you listen, you're attempting to understand people's perspectives while showing them deference and respect.
- People rarely open up about their lives without being asked good questions by people who are genuinely interested in them.

The five characteristics of good listeners are:

1. Good listening is much more than being silent while the other person talks.

2. Good listening includes interactions that build a person's self-esteem.

3. Good listening is a cooperative conversation.

4. Good listeners tend to make suggestions.

5. Good listeners demonstrate empathy.

 MEMORY VERSE:

James 1:19: *"Everyone should be quick to listen, slow to speak, and slow to become angry."*

A PRAYER:

Heavenly Father, I ask You to give me ears to listen to people, not only to what they say, but also to what they don't say. Help me to pay attention, make eye contact, ask good questions, and really listen to people. Give me opportunities to have conversations with each of the five people I am praying for. Teach me how to listen in a way that makes them feel valued, seen, and heard. Help me hear what the Spirit would say to them in the moment. I continue to pray that You would make Yourself known to _____, _____, _____, _____, and _____.

 SELF-REFLECTION QUESTIONS:

1. After reading this chapter, in what areas do you need to grow to become a good listener?
2. What is the most important lesson about listening that you learned from Jesus' interaction with the woman at the well?
3. Think about your five. Do you make them feel seen and heard? Are you listening to them with empathy? Does your input leave them feeling inspired and hopeful?

 CALL TO ACTION:

Can you set up a time to talk to at least one of your five this week? It could be a phone call, a walk around the neighborhood, a coffee break at the office, etc. Review the qualities of a good listener prior to your conversation and practice listening to that person share their stories and heart. Ask God to give you the right words to communicate not just your opinion on matters, but your care and concern for them.

EAT WITH THEM

*"Ask not what you can do for your country.
Ask what's for lunch. "*[55]

— Orson Welles

I still remember how my blood boiled as I followed the news of a city ordinance in Albuquerque, New Mexico. Ken, one of our civic leaders, helped pass the ordinance, which I believed was both unconstitutional and unbiblical. While I had been frustrated with many of Ken's decisions over the years, this one sent me over the edge.

As I drove down the road and squeezed the steering wheel angrily, I prayed, "God, please remove Ken from office and replace him with a godly leader!"

I thought I was praying a God-honoring prayer. But the instant the words left my mouth, I felt the Holy Spirit's rebuke: "Brian, you have never prayed for Ken with love in your heart. Before asking me to remove him from office, try befriending him."

I released the death grip on my steering wheel while blinking slowly. I was dumbfounded.

That's not just a random thought in my head, is it?

"Lord, are You serious?" I finally whispered. God didn't say anything, but the feeling of His rebuke continued to pierce my heart. Still reeling from God's words, I pulled my car over to the shoulder of the road.

"God, I know You love everyone, including Ken. But can't You just remove him from office? Why do I have to reach out to him?"

The feeling in my spirit only intensified.

"Okay, Lord. I'll try, but You know this will not be easy. And many Christian leaders in this city will criticize me if I befriend him."

I ran my hands through my hair and sighed.

I felt the Spirit prompting me to invite Ken to lunch. If I procrastinated, I knew I would talk myself out of it, so I swallowed my pride and called Ken's assistant. I asked her if she could schedule a lunch appointment for me with Ken.

That day, I began praying for Ken by name every day. I no longer prayed judgment on him but God's love, mercy, and grace. I met Ken at a small Mexican restaurant near his office a week later.

"Thank you for inviting me to lunch, Pastor Alarid," Ken said as he browsed over the menu. "I've heard great things about you and New Mexico Prays. Thank you for your leadership here in our community. It is a blessing to get to know you personally."

I smiled and took a deep breath.

"Thank you, Ken. That's kind of you to say. And I want to express my gratitude for…for…(I was struggling to bring myself to the words I knew God wanted me to say)…your leadership to our city.

"I'm sure we disagree about many issues, but I bet we have more in common than we both realize," I continued. "I want you to know that I pray for you every day. I would love to be your friend and work with you to make Albuquerque a better city for everyone to live in."

That first lunch lasted several hours, and though it wasn't easy, we made a genuine heart connection.

Over the next three years, we built a close friendship, and to my surprise, Ken became one of my biggest supporters. I invited him to join us for our Convoy of Hope outreach, and he came. Later that fall, Ken joined us in feeding 2,500 families for Thanksgiving at Albuquerque Public Schools. He stayed until we distributed the last bag of groceries.

Spring arrived, and Ken joined us for the National Day of Prayer at Civic Plaza, where over 2,000 people gathered for worship and prayer. During our group prayer, I prayed with Ken and another city counselor. As I prayed for God to bless Ken and pour His love upon him, he began crying, and I felt his tears drop on my hand. I started crying, too. I knew God was touching his heart, even though his politics and lifestyle hadn't changed yet.

Ken persuaded the Albuquerque City Council to donate $30,000 for one of our outreaches. When a delegation of Chinese priests and diplomats visited our city, Ken and I hosted them, along with my friends, Lt. Governor John Sanchez and Archbishop John Wester.

Two months later, we hosted Love ABQ, which served the city with over 3,000 volunteer hours. Ken served alongside me, Calvary Church, and hundreds of believers. A few evangelical leaders condemned me for befriending Ken, but I knew Jesus had called me to be his friend. And I could see his heart slowly changing.

One cool October morning, with hot air balloons spread across the Albuquerque skyline, Ken called me.

"Pastor Alarid, can I take you to lunch tomorrow? I need to talk to you."

We met at his favorite Mexican restaurant. I could see a new excitement in his eyes.

"Pastor Alarid, I've been thinking a lot about my faith recently. I was baptized as an infant. And I've been to church off and on over the years. But I feel something different when I'm with you. What is it?"

I smiled.

"Thank you, Ken. That feeling inside your heart is Jesus drawing you to Himself. Jesus loves you, Ken, and He died to give you joy, peace, and eternal life. I know you know a lot about Jesus, but have you ever put your faith in Jesus for salvation?"

"No, I don't think so."

"Do you want to?"

Ken nodded his head.

And there, over a bowl of chips and salsa, Ken put his faith in Jesus. He had been exposed to Jesus and the church, but he put his trust in Jesus for the first time that day. It was one of the best days of my life. We talked about ways we could serve together to improve our city, like two boys dreaming about building a tree fort.

We were two men from different backgrounds, united by God for the good of the city. That's what Jeremiah 29:7 is all about—seeking the peace and prosperity of your city.

I wish the story had ended there.

Two weeks later, Ken suffered a severe stroke. On Christmas Eve 2019, Ken's assistant called me and asked if I would come to the hospital the day after Christmas to pray for him.

I cried all the way to the hospital. When I grabbed Ken's hand, he opened his eyes and turned his head toward me. He couldn't speak, but he squeezed my hand three times. There was a look of peace in Ken's eyes as he faced eternity.

Ken's assistant called me three days later while I was driving from Albuquerque to Oklahoma. She had bad news. Ken had passed from this life into the next. I pulled our vehicle over and wept for an hour in the parking lot of a gas station.

What if I hadn't responded to God's whisper and reached out to Ken? What if I hadn't been willing to overlook our political differences to befriend him? Why did it take me so long to become his friend?

I realized my religious pride kept me away from Ken for twenty years. We only had three years together. It was way too short. I wish I had reached out to him years before.

The day Ken passed away, I told God I would never let religious or political differences keep me from loving people again. I promised God I would always carry Ken in my heart. Since then, I have tried to love people who think and vote differently than me.

What's my point?

What if the people you dislike are those God is calling you to love and serve? What if they become the very people who help you become a better follower of Jesus? What if the miracle you are seeking is right in front of you, hidden in plain sight, disguised as people you don't care for? Can you hear the Savior's voice telling you to walk across the room, love them, and serve them?

Before I met with Ken for the first time at that Mexican restaurant, I wanted nothing to do with him and was content to resent him from a distance. But God moved in my heart to pray for him. The more I prayed for him, the more I loved him. The more we broke bread together, the closer our friendship grew. And through it all, his heart softened and opened toward the Gospel.

Take advantage of every opportunity to love people. You never know how much time you will have with them. I still miss Ken and often cry over losing him, but I find comfort in knowing we will meet one day again at the marriage supper of the Lamb. I'll sit across the table from Ken, and we'll share another bowl of chips and salsa. And then we'll raise our glasses and toast King Jesus, who saved us both!

Never underestimate the power of breaking bread with people. Food has a magical ability to break down walls and open people's hearts. I won Ken to Christ one *enchilada* at a time.

At the Table with Jesus

The third habit in the B.L.E.S.S. lifestyle is to *eat with them.* This is my favorite part of evangelism. As you have been praying for people and listening to them, also take the time to share a meal with them, just as I did with Ken.

Jesus said in Luke 7:34, *"The Son of Man has come eating and drinking, and you say, 'Look at him! A glutton and a drunkard, a friend of tax collectors and sinners!'"* Eating with people far from God was such an integral part of His life that His critics tried to use it against Him. They said, "All this guy does is eat and drink!"

Jesus spent an excessive amount of time eating with people far from God. It was His secret to winning their hearts. The Gospels reveal Jesus as a highly relational leader who loved breaking bread with people. In the Gospel of Luke, you can find Jesus either at a meal, on His way to a meal, or on His way back from a meal.

In his book, *A Meal With Jesus*, Tim Chester makes this brilliant observation: "Jesus spent his time eating and drinking—a lot of his time. He was a party animal. His mission strategy was a long meal, stretching into the evening. He did evangelism and discipleship 'round a table with some grilled fish, a loaf of bread, and a pitcher of wine."[56]

In Luke 5, Jesus was walking through the streets of Capernaum when He encountered a Roman tax collector named Levi. Tax collectors were Roman employees who collected taxes for the empire. On top of the exorbitant taxes Rome demanded, many tax collectors would add a personal fee. Effectively, the tax collectors were becoming rich by stealing from the Jews. That's why the Jews hated tax collectors like Levi (also known as Matthew).

But that didn't stop Jesus. As He passed by Levi's booth, Jesus stopped and said to Levi, "Follow Me."

Levi promptly left everything behind and followed Jesus. That evening, Levi threw an extravagant dinner party at his house with Jesus, His disciples, and all of Levi's friends: tax

CHAPTER 5

collectors, swindlers, and sinners. The Pharisees challenged Jesus, asking: "Why do you eat and drink with tax collectors and sinners?" Jesus answered, "Those who are well have no need of a physician, but those who are sick. I have not come to call the righteous but sinners to repentance." (Luke 5:30-31)

Jesus went to dinner at Levi's house because it was the ideal place to connect with sinners. Are you willing to take a risk and eat with sinners?

In Luke 19, a wealthy tax collector named Zacchaeus from Jericho came to listen to Jesus preach. Because he was short, he couldn't see Jesus over the enormous crowd. (I can relate to that!) In a desperate move, he climbed a sycamore tree so he could finally lay eyes on Jesus.

Jesus saw him and yelled, "Zacchaeus, come down! We're having a party at your house tonight!"

Zacchaeus was surprised.

"What do You mean?" he shouted back.

Jesus replied, "I'm coming to your home for dinner, and I'm going to stay the night with you as well."

Zacchaeus was blown away. *The Messiah wants to have dinner with a sinner like me, at my house?*

When Zacchaeus climbed down the tree, he said, "Look, Lord! Here and now, I give half of my possessions to the poor, and if I have cheated anybody out of anything, I will pay back four times the amount." He repented right there on the spot.

Jesus smiled and said, "Today, salvation has come to this house because this man, too, is a son of Abraham. For the

Son of Man came to seek and to save the lost." This invitation
to have dinner with Jesus radically changed Zacchaeus' life
before they even sat at the table.

When you invite people to share a meal, you communicate
you value them. To eat, it's been said, is to enter intimately
into the lives of others. Before you ask people to attend
church with you, why don't you invite them to your home or
a restaurant to share a meal?

Tim Chester shares this powerful insight: "So the meals
of Jesus represent something bigger…Food is stuff. It's not
ideas. It's not theories. It's, well, it's food, and you put it
in your mouth, taste it, and eat it. And meals are more than
food. They're social occasions. They represent friendship,
community, and welcome."[57]

Build Experiences Together

Eating together is fundamental to building experiences
with others. You can't hike a mountain or sail across the
Pacific with everyone, but you can eat with them. Sharing a
meal is one of the easiest ways to build a relationship. That's
why romantic and business relationships often begin with
lunch or dinner. Sharing a meal helps you go beyond polite
conversation and connect at a deeper level.

I remember sitting with Mercy and some friends at an
ocean-side restaurant in the Italian port city of Livorno, on
the west coast of Tuscany. There was a cool summer breeze,
and the smell of olive oil and spices was in the air.

CHAPTER 5

As I scanned the menu, my friend, Dante Bernaducci, assured me that Livorno had the freshest shrimp in Italy. We swapped stories, shared appetizers, and laughed while waiting for dinner. Mercy and I were having the time of our lives.

That is, until my platter of jumbo shrimp arrived. Their eyes were staring at me, and their antennae were pointing at me as if they were taunting me. I was expecting the peeled shrimp you buy at the grocery store, not these lifelike creatures still encased in their outer shell. How was I supposed to eat them? Where would I even start?

It took me about ten minutes to peel my first shrimp and detach all its legs and whiskers. I made an absolute mess all over the table before giving up. My friend, Bruno, gave me dirty looks from across the table for not eating the shrimp.

And that's when it happened.

Dante said, "It looks like you are having trouble. Let me help you!" Dante grabbed a prawn and began peeling and cleaning it, explaining the process. Over the next several minutes, Dante shelled all the shrimp on my plate.

This simple act of brotherly love at a Tuscan restaurant transformed my thoughts about food and friendship. At the dinner table, we became brothers for life. I can't think of anything else that could have enabled us to bond so quickly and deeply. As we enjoy flavors together, we let down our guard, relax, and invite others into our lives. Italian chef Giada De Laurentiis noted, "Food brings people together on many levels. It's the nourishment of the soul and body; it's truly love."[58]

Call to Action

Here is my challenge: You eat about twenty-one meals every week, more or less. Can you share one of those meals with someone far from God? If you can't do it weekly, how about every two weeks or even monthly?

If you don't have a spacious home to host people, that's okay. The goal isn't to impress people but to spend time with them. During our first year of marriage, Mercy and I lived in a 300-square-foot apartment in upstate New York. We made $7,200 yearly—before taxes, tithes, and a steady supply of Coca-Cola and Doritos.

But even though we were poor and lived in a tiny apartment, we hosted people at least twice a week. We couldn't afford to make dinner for our guests, so we served them drinks and snacks.

A few years later, God blessed us with a 600-square-foot guest house in Albuquerque. At first, we had no furniture in our living room until Mercy found a hideous sofa in a garbage dumpster and claimed it. It was saturated with stains, but she covered it with an embroidered blanket someone had given us for our wedding. It wasn't fancy, but people no longer had to sit on the floor!

When God blessed us with our first home in 2005, we promised Him to use our house to host people. Over the past twenty-six years of marriage, we've hosted over 2,500 meals and coffees in our various apartments and homes.

Meals are the bread and butter of discipleship—*pun intended.* I've witnessed more spiritual transformations take place over a meal than in any church service. You always have more influence with friends than strangers, and the quickest way to make friends is to share a meal.

> **You always have more influence with friends than with strangers, and the quickest way to make friends is to share a meal.**

Civil rights activist César Chávez said, "If you really want to make a friend, go to someone's house and eat with him...The people who give you their food give you their heart."[59]

Take a moment to pray and ask God to show you the people He wants you to share a meal with over the next few months. Reach out to them and schedule a time to connect.

Make time in your weekly calendar for people far from God. If you don't put it in your schedule, it won't happen. Who are you going to share a meal with this week?

Chapter 5: Takeaways

 KEY POINTS:

- Jesus spent an excessive amount of time eating with people far from God. It was His secret to winning their hearts. The Gospels reveal Jesus as a highly relational leader who loved breaking bread with people.
- Food has a magical ability to break down walls and open people's hearts.
- Meals are the bread and butter of discipleship.
- What if the miracle you are seeking is right in front of you, disguised as people you don't care for?
- Eating together helps you build experiences with others. Sharing a meal helps you go beyond polite conversation and connect at a deeper level.
- You always have more influence with friends than with strangers, and the quickest way to make friends is to share a meal.
- On average, you eat about twenty-one meals per week. What if you share one of those meals with someone who needs Jesus?

 MEMORY VERSE:

Luke 5:30-32: "But the Pharisees and the teachers of the law who belonged to their sect complained to his disciples, 'Why do you eat and drink with tax collectors and sinners?' Jesus answered them, 'It is not the healthy who need a doctor, but the sick. I have not come to call the righteous, but sinners to repentance.'"

A PRAYER:

Lord, help me to redeem the time and be willing to share meals with people far from You. No matter how different or how difficult they are, give me opportunities to share a meal with each of the five people I am praying for daily. I pray that as we eat together, walls would come down and opportunities to share Your love would abound during our time together.

 SELF-REFLECTION QUESTIONS:

1. Think about a time when sharing a meal with others broke down walls between you and them. How can sharing a meal with someone far from God help their walls come down and deepen relationships?

2. What might have happened if Brian had let political differences keep him from eating with Ken? Do you have someone in your life who you vehemently disagree with politically or philosophically? What would it take to invite that person over for a meal?

 CALL TO ACTION:

You've already written the names of five people you will be praying for on a daily basis. How about making a plan to share a snack, a meal, or even dessert with each of them? Stop right now and reach out to at least one of the five and schedule a time to eat together this week or next week. If you don't calendar it, it won't happen.

CHAPTER 6

SERVE THEM

"Everybody can be great...because anybody can serve.
You don't have to have a college degree to serve.
You don't have to make your subject and verb agree to serve.
You only need a heart full of grace. A soul generated by love."[60]

— **Martin Luther King, Jr.**

"Baby, I'm going to pick up one of my college students for church. Can we take her with us to lunch after the service?" Mercy batted her eyelashes, and I was powerless to resist.

"Sure, sounds like fun," I said, but I was in for an enormous surprise! After preaching, I drove to an upscale Chinese restaurant in our local mall. Mercy and her student were already seated at a table when I arrived.

"Hi, I'm Brian! What's your name?" I said, offering my hand across the table to the young lady. She seemed uncertain about me but shook my hand anyway.

"I'm Snoop."

"As in Snoop Dogg?" I asked.

"Yeah. My name's Charlycia, but everyone calls me Snoop."

"That's cool!" I said. "My friends and family call me *White Chocolate*." (And by friends and family, I mean only my daughter Lauren.)

91

CHAPTER 6

"White Chocolate? Okay. That's different. Why do they call you White Chocolate?" she asked, raising her eyebrows as high as possible. Out of the corner of my eye, I saw Mercy drop her face into her palm in embarrassment, but I didn't care.

"Well, when I was a basketball player in high school, my jump shot was as smooth as, well, you know…white chocolate." I winked and added, "And when I was a rapper, my stage name was White Chocolate!"

Not even a grin. Snoop wasn't impressed.

I laughed awkwardly and tried to move the conversation along.

"So, where are you from?"

Snoop sighed. "I'm from Queens in New York City."

"Oh, that's awesome! I'm from Los Angeles, but I love New York. West Coast to East Coast! That's what's up!"

Snoop looked at me with a dull expression as if to say, *Stop! Just stop.*

"Uh, anyhow…" I scrambled my brain for something better than cheesy jokes. "So, tell me your story?"

"Excuse me?"

"You know, what's your story? Tell me about yourself."

Snoop folded her arms and leaned back in her chair.

"Why do you want to hear my story?" she said defensively. "I don't even know you. Why are you trying to get up in my business?"

"Well, you're my wife's student, we're eating lunch together, and I want to get to know you," I said, a bit taken aback. Then I tried again, "Tell me about your family."

Snoop squinted at me and shook her head in disbelief.

"You really can't take a hint, can you? Why are you asking so many [bleep]-ing questions?"

The tension was palpable.

"Hello, everyone! Can I take your order?"

The waiter appeared out of nowhere with a pen and notepad, and quickly realized he had walked into a terribly awkward moment. We each gave him our orders, and I tried resuming our conversation. But everything went downhill from there, so I'll spare you the details. Shortly after our food arrived, I decided to escape.

"It was great to meet you, Snoop. Thanks for coming to lunch with us."

I turned to Mercy and said, "I'm going to take Chloe and Colin to a movie." She knew I was bailing out on her, but I just could not take any more of her new friend's attitude.

Exit stage right.

As I watched an animated movie with my kids, I fumed over what had just transpired.

Why did she become so upset? I was only trying to be nice. Oh, well, at least I won't see her again.

A few weeks later, Mercy said to me, "Guess who I'm picking up for church today?"

I looked at her with pleading eyes. "Please, not that rude student of yours."

"Honey, don't be like that! Give her a chance. She's hurting and needs people who will just love her."

I sighed, trying to reconcile my feelings. But I was skeptical, very skeptical.

After service, Snoop shouted at me in front of everyone in the church lobby. "Hey, White Chocolate! Your outfit is on point today. And your message was pretty decent, too."

Decent? Well, at least she had an eye for fashion.

Several weeks passed before Mercy told me Snoop was visiting our church again. After the service, Mercy gave me *the look.* (If you are married, you know exactly which look I'm talking about.) She told me we were having Snoop over for lunch and that I needed to be on my best behavior.

Yes, Boss!

That was the first time we hosted Snoop in our home. Little did I know it would be the beginning of something special. We ate one of Mercy's gourmet meals: chicken cordon bleu, mashed potatoes, and salad tossed in a homemade balsamic dressing. Then we watched a movie with our kids. Snoop's boisterous laugh was so contagious that our whole family laughed along with her until our stomachs hurt. From then on, lunch with Snoop became a weekly affair.

A year later, Snoop devoted her life to Jesus, and soon after that, she asked me to baptize her in water. She was making huge strides as a disciple of Christ.

One evening, Mercy dropped a bomb on me. Snoop was struggling financially, and the electricity in her apartment had been turned off. Mercy asked, "Can Snoop stay with us until she recovers financially? We can't let her go back to her apartment knowing she has no lights or air conditioning."

"Are you serious, Babe? We have three kids, and we don't have a spare bedroom unless you count the closet!"

"We'll make room," Mercy insisted.

I had intended to pray and explain to God why this was a bad idea, but before I could, the Holy Spirit moved on my heart and gave me the compassion I needed.

We welcomed Snoop into our home the next day. With no guest bedroom, our daughter, Chloe, gave Snoop her room and shared a room with her sister, Lauren. The kids were excited about having Snoop at home all the time.

After dinner, I laid out some ground rules for Snoop. "You can live with us rent-free for as long as you need, but you need to be here at 8 p.m. for family devotions and help with chores around the house. If you live with us, we will treat you like family."

As the months went by, Snoop truly became part of our family. We ate together, prayed together, played games, watched movies, and laughed together. Our kids started looking to her as their older sister, and she embraced that role. We fought for each other and sometimes even fought each other. But that's what families do.

Four months later, Snoop asked if we could have a serious sit-down talk. Nothing could have prepared me for what she was about to say.

"I have a biological dad and a stepfather, who I really love. But you have become really important to me, so I want to ask you something. Would you be my dad?"

I took a deep breath and leaned in, the corners of my eyes growing moist. "Charlycia," I said, using her birth name, "I would be honored to be your dad!"

Snoop smiled with tears in her eyes.

"You, Mercy, Chloe, Colin, and Lauren are my family. And I love you like a father." She laughed sheepishly. "Can I call you 'Pops'?"

I laughed, too.

"Of course you can call me Pops. Or even White Chocolate if you want."

"Pops will be just fine," she said, rolling her eyes.

Years have passed since that time, and I have watched Snoop blossom into an incredible human being—intelligent, generous, faithful, fiercely loyal, hard-working, and devoted. She has faced challenges and heartaches and has never given up. Her faith has been tested and shaken, but she has remained faithful.

Snoop taught me that nothing communicates love as much as service. We won Snoop's heart through love, service, friendship, kindness, and generosity. We prayed for her, cared for her, and shared Jesus with her. And the Father drew her to His Son.

I have three biological children and an adopted daughter named Snoop. Her love has changed my life and our love has changed hers. She has made me a better person. *I love you, Snoop. Blood in, blood out.*

Love Moves Us to Action

The fourth habit in the B.L.E.S.S. lifestyle is to serve them. As you pray for people, listen to them, and eat with them, also look for opportunities to serve them. If you ask them good questions and really listen to their story, the needs in their lives will become apparent. When you become aware of their need, find ways to either meet it or connect them to someone who can. If you can't do a lot, do a little. But do something. The fastest way to win people's hearts is to serve them.

In his book, *Love Does*, author Bob Goff writes, "Love is never stationary. In the end, love doesn't just keep thinking about it or keep planning for it. Simply put: love does."[61]

I love that simple idea—*love does*. Love compels you to serve people in need. Love moved the Good Samaritan to do something for the man who was robbed, beaten, and left for dead. He bandaged his wounds, gave him wine and oil, put him on his donkey, took him to an inn, and paid for his stay there until he recovered (Luke 10).

Love is more than feeling sorry for people—it's actually helping them. Be honest: How many times have you seen a TV commercial showing starving children in Africa, and you quickly changed the channel? I've done it, too! You felt sorry for them but you weren't willing to donate money just yet. Feeling sorry for hungry kids is easier than helping them. But genuine love is not passive—it's active. Love is more than emotion, sentiment, or feeling—it's action.

Love *cares*.
Love *gives*.
Love *heals*.
Love *washes*.
Love *feeds*.
Love *serves*.

CHAPTER 6

James 2:16 illustrates this well: *"Dear friends, do you think you'll get anywhere in this if you learn all the right words but never do anything? Does merely talking about faith indicate that a person really has it?*

For instance, you come upon an old friend dressed in rags and half-starved and say, 'Good morning, friend! Be clothed in Christ! Be filled with the Holy Spirit!' and walk off without providing so much as a coat or a cup of soup—where does that get you? Isn't it obvious that God-talk without God-acts is outrageous nonsense?"[62]

If people are hungry, feed them. If they are homeless, give them shelter. If they are unemployed, help them find a job. If they are sick, care for them. If they are cold, provide them with a jacket and blanket. There are always variables to these opportunities to serve, but true love will overcome them and do what is needed.

Nobody has ever had a bigger claim to privilege than Jesus, but He chose the lowly path of a servant. Instead of powering up, Jesus powered down. And He won people's hearts by serving them and meeting their needs. Jesus is the greatest servant of all time.

Paul illustrates this in Philippians 2:5-8: *"In your relationships with one another, have the same mindset as Christ Jesus: Who, being in very nature God, did not consider equality with God something to be used to his own advantage; rather, he made himself nothing by taking the very nature of a servant, being made in human likeness. And being found in appearance as a man, he humbled himself by becoming obedient to death—even death on a cross!"*

Jesus abandoned the glories of heaven and came to Earth to serve us. Although He had limitless power, Jesus chose to serve. That's the hallmark of servant leaders—they put the needs of others first. Jesus saw serving people as His mission in life. He came to serve, not to be served.

People don't care how much you *know* until they know how much you *care*. It's not enough to tell people that Jesus loves them. That's not the question they're asking. In their time of need, they are asking for a plate of food, shoes to wear, a job opportunity, a tutor, or a visit to their hospital room. And when you show up, when you give, and when you serve, they will know they are loved without you even saying a word.

Jesus said in Matthew 5:16, *"In the same way, let your light shine before men, that they may see your good deeds and praise your Father in heaven."* People often need to see your good works before they will believe in your witness. The predominant human attitude is, "What's in it for *me*?" Whereas Jesus' attitude was, "What's in it for *you*?"

We are hard-wired only to do things that obviously benefit us. It takes a radical encounter with Christ to transform us from being self-serving into being unselfish servants who seek the benefit of others before ourselves.

Jesus didn't come to be served—He came to serve others, saying in Matthew 20:25-28, *"You know that the rulers of the Gentiles lord it over them, and their high officials exercise authority over them. Not so with you.*

"Instead, whoever wants to become great among you must be your servant, and whoever wants to be first must be

your slave—just as the Son of Man did not come to be served, but to serve, and to give his life as a ransom for many." If serving is *beneath* you, leading is *above* you. It's that simple. The greatest leaders are the most devoted servants. They are shaped and formed by serving, away from the limelight.

> **If serving is beneath you, leading is above you.**

Wanted: Foot Washer

Then he said, "Do you understand what I have done to you? You address me as 'Teacher' and 'Master,' and rightly so. That is what I am. So if I, the Master and Teacher, washed your feet, you must now wash each other's feet. I've laid down a pattern for you. What I've done, you do. I'm only pointing out the obvious. A servant is not ranked above his master; an employee doesn't give orders to the employer. If you understand what I'm telling you, act like it—and live a blessed life."[63] — John 13:12-17

Jesus gave the disciples a clear and lasting image of being a servant at the last supper.

"Peter and John, I have an important assignment for you," Jesus said. "I want you to prepare everything for us to celebrate the Passover meal together."

Peter, always the first to speak, replied, "We got you covered, Lord. Consider it done."

John and Peter sat down and made a checklist.

Passover lamb ✓
Water ✓
Wine ✓
Bread ✓
Upper room ✓
Table and thirteen chairs ✓
Basin ✓
Towel ✓

After Jesus celebrated the Passover meal with His disciples, He did something nobody saw coming. Jesus stood up, walked across the room, and poured water into a basin.

I'm sure Peter thought, *We already have enough wine to drink. I wonder why Jesus is bringing us water.*

And then Jesus did the *unthinkable*—He knelt before them and washed their feet. The Ruler of the Universe became a lowly foot washer! At that moment, Peter and John realized they had forgotten one small but very important detail. In ancient civilizations, it was customary to provide guests who visited your home with a servant to wash their feet. Or, at the bare minimum, they would give their guests a pitcher of water to clean their feet.

Sandals were the primary footwear in those days. After walking on unpaved, harsh roads, a person's feet would become dirty, often with minor cuts and bruises. Despite their meticulous planning and careful execution, Peter and John somehow forgot to find a servant to wash their feet.

Jesus didn't complain about their oversight. He simply washed their feet to model for His followers the posture and nature of a servant. A servant does whatever is needed, which in this case, was foot washing.

Was washing feet Jesus's primary calling in life? Of course not. But that didn't stop Him from doing it. Jesus washed dirty, stinky feet because they needed to be washed. Servants meet real needs at the right time.

Servants are like duct tape. I bet you have a roll or two at home. It is a cloth-backed pressure-sensitive tape often coated with polyethylene and has a million uses. Race car drivers use it to repair fiberglass bodywork. It can prevent you from bleeding to death. The military uses it to repair jeeps, firearms, and aircraft.

Duct tape was even used on the Apollo 13 and Apollo 17 space shuttles to make repairs, saving the lives of the astronauts onboard. One of my childhood heroes, *MacGyver*, always carried a flattened roll of duct tape in his back pocket in case of an emergency. And he used it to escape from all sorts of jams, build airplanes, and hold down pressure plates.

My point is that duct tape can do anything. In the same way, servants are flexible, adaptable, and willing to do whatever is needed. No task is too large or too small for servants. They finish the job without complaining or seeking the praise of man.

Called to Serve

We all have different gifts, callings, and destinies, but the foundation of our calling is servanthood. Peter said in 1 Peter 4:10, "Each of you should use whatever gift you have received to serve others as faithful stewards of God's grace in its various forms."

The gifts and talents God gave you aren't for you to showcase your talent but to serve people. Your gifts aren't *about* you or *for* you. They are for the glory of God and the service of people. If you serve people with a humble heart, God will promote you. Don't worry about your platform. Focus on serving people, and Jesus will exalt you in due time and give you a platform.

The Apostle Paul wrote in Philippians 1:1, *"This letter is from Paul and Timothy, servants of Christ Jesus."* Paul found his primary identity as a servant of Jesus Christ. His gifting as an apostle was secondary. This heart posture is what God wants from us as well.

Jesus said in Matthew 25:37-40: "Then the righteous will answer him, 'Lord, when did we see you hungry and feed you, or thirsty and give you something to drink? When did we see you a stranger and invite you in, or needing clothes and clothe you? When did we see you sick or in prison and go to visit you?' "The King will reply, 'Truly I tell you, whatever you did for one of the least of these brothers and sisters of mine, you did for me.'"

Mother Teresa personified the essence of unselfish service. She devoted fifty years to serving the poor and caring for the sick in India, enduring the harshest conditions.

What inspired her to devote her life to service? She testified, "Every person is Jesus in disguise. I see Jesus in every human being. I say to myself, 'This is hungry Jesus, I must feed him. This is sick Jesus. This one has leprosy or gangrene; I must wash him and tend to him.' I serve because I love Jesus."[64]

Meeting people's felt needs opens their hearts for us to minister to their spiritual needs. As William Booth, the founder of the Salvation Army, said, "You cannot warm the hearts of people with God's love if they have an empty stomach and cold feet."[65]

Call to Action

When you meet people's physical needs, you also restore their dignity. You are saying to them, "You are valuable. You are worthy of love. You are worthy of food, clothing, and shelter because you were made in the image of God. Jesus loves you and so do I."

Simple acts of service are profound demonstrations of love. That's because a hug is more than physical touch.

A bag of groceries is more than food.

A winter jacket is more than warmth.

A place to stay is more than shelter.

And a job is more than money.

Every person you will ever meet is Jesus in disguise. Will you serve them with His love and compassion, as if you were serving Jesus in the flesh? Will you meet their needs and offer them hope in Christ?

Who are you going to serve this week?

Chapter 6: Takeaways

 KEY POINTS:

At the last supper, Jesus taught us by example what it means to become a servant to all. He did not demand to be served but washed His disciples' feet to model the posture and nature of a servant.

If serving is beneath you, leading is above you.

People often need to see your good works before they will believe in your witness.

Servants are like duct tape. They are willing to do whatever is needed.

Meeting people's felt needs opens their hearts for us to minister to their spiritual needs.

Serving others is the fastest way to win their hearts.

People don't care how much you know until they know how much you care.

God gave us gifts to serve others, and our service prepares their hearts for the Gospel.

 MEMORY VERSE:

1 Peter 4:10: *"Each of you should use whatever gift you have received to serve others as faithful stewards of God's grace in its various forms."*

A PRAYER:

Lord, give me a servant's heart. Thank You for calling me to be a blessing to the five people I've been praying for daily. Give me eyes that see their needs and a heart to serve willingly. Help me to use the gifts and resources You have given me to show them Your love in action. Continue to work in their hearts and draw them closer to You.

 SELF-REFLECTION QUESTIONS:

1. Do an inventory of your life. Are you currently serving others by ministering to their practical needs?

2. As you pray, listen, and eat with your five, what needs do you see in their lives that you can meet?

3. What gifts has God given you that would help you meet those needs?

4. If their needs are beyond your resources and giftings, who can you partner with to meet them?

5. Is there someone in your circle of influence you can connect them with so their need can be met?

 CALL TO ACTION:

Make a list of the needs you see in the lives of the five people you are praying for daily. Ask God which needs you can personally meet or who you know who might be able to meet their needs. As you think through meeting those needs, make sure you prioritize protecting people's privacy, dignity, and autonomy.

CHAPTER 7

SHARE JESUS

*"To be a soul winner is the happiest thing in this world.
And with every soul you bring to Jesus Christ,
you seem to get a new heaven here upon earth."*[66]

— **Charles Spurgeon**

The doorbell rang.

I opened my front door, and there he was—Bible in hand, backpack strapped to his shoulder, and eyes that could barely contain his excitement. This young man had tearfully accepted Jesus at our church three weeks before. Since then, he'd been coming to my house every Wednesday, hungry to study the Gospel of John with me.

"Hey, bro! Come on in," I said.

But this time, he wasn't alone. His girlfriend followed him as he made his way into my living room. I noticed her black clothes matched her black lipstick, eye shadow, and jewelry.

Mercy looked her up and down and smiled.

"I love your style!" she said. In her *Depeche Mode* days, Mercy used to dress just like her.

There's nothing wrong with wearing all black, but there was something off about this girl. I couldn't put my finger on it at first, but as she walked past me and followed her boyfriend into my office, I felt a dark presence over her, and then a revelation hit me.

I leaned close to Mercy and whispered, "This girl is a witch."

"Don't talk like that, Brian!"

Mercy scolded me, thinking that I was making a bad joke about her Gothic style.

I shook my head.

"I'm not making fun of her. I mean it. I think she's a practicing witch."

I glanced through the door and saw the young man rummaging through his backpack for his Bible and notebook while his girlfriend played with her phone.

I looked back to Mercy and said, "Pray for us. I've got a feeling this Bible study is going to be eventful!"

I stepped through the door to my home office and sat down. As I opened my Bible, I glanced up at the girl. She met my eyes with disgust and hatred. It was like looking into the Eye of Sauron for a split second.

I was so unnerved that I lost my train of thought and had to look down to compose myself.

As providence had it, we were studying John chapter 3 that week. I explained the importance of being born-again and talked about God's love for the world, described so beautifully in John 3:16: *"For God so loved the world that he gave his one and only Son, that whoever believes in him shall not perish but have eternal life."*

The young lady laughed when we read that.

"You Christians are stupid and gullible," she said mockingly, looking up at me.

I looked up from the pages of my Bible.

"You're saying God showed His love for us by sending His Son to be tortured to death? That's the dumbest thing I've ever heard. What kind of loving Father would murder His Son for complete strangers? Are you even listening to yourself?"

She rolled her eyes and laughed again. Her boyfriend was speechless and nervously looked at me to see how I would respond.

I took a deep breath and chose to overlook her offense before responding.

"Well, that's exactly the point," I said. "God's love for us is so radically different from human love that we can't comprehend it. God sacrificed His Son Jesus for us because He loves us."

She squinted and shook her head as if that was the most ridiculous thing she'd ever heard.

"That's crazy!" she shouted. "That's not love; that's evil. If God loved us, why didn't *He* die for us? Why did He murder His Son? Your God is a coward and a fraud. That's why I'm a Wiccan."

Oh, snap! She really was a witch. My Spidey senses were right!

By this point, her boyfriend looked like he wanted to bolt and never return, but she was merely warming up for what came next.

"You have children, don't you? Would you kill any of them for me, my boyfriend, or anyone else?"

"Yes, I have three kids. And no, I wouldn't sacrifice any of them for you or even my best friend, Bruno. I understand where you're coming from though. But since I am a parent, I can also understand in a small way the incredible sacrifice God made for us. As a parent, you suffer more when your kids are in pain than when you are in pain. Sacrificing His only Son cost the Father everything. That was the greatest demonstration of love in history. He did what no one else would ever do—He gave His only Son for you and me."

"Then I guess He loved everyone else more than His Son. That makes Him a pretty terrible father if you ask me."

"I see how it could seem that way at first, but you're missing one important detail: Jesus chose to lay down His life for you and me. The Father didn't force Him to do anything. Jesus willingly came to Earth to die on the cross for our sins because He loves us and wants us to spend eternity with Him. I know you don't see it right now, but Jesus loves you, and I pray that one day you will open your heart to His love."

She hurled a few choice words in my direction, stormed out of my office, and slammed the door. Her boyfriend stared at me with a deer-in-the-headlights look as if to say, "What in the world just happened?"

I looked him in the eyes and tried to get his attention.

"Dude, that girl is trouble! She will pull you away from Christ if you don't break up with her as fast as possible."

He looked down, shook his head, and apologized for his girlfriend's outburst. "See you next week," he said as he picked up his backpack and left my office.

He returned several times after that incident, but I saw him go through a vicious cycle over the next few years. He would break up with his girlfriend and serve Jesus, then return to her and backslide. Repeatedly, he struggled to let go of her and remain faithful to Jesus.

Through it all, I continued to pray for her, hoping against hope that someday, somewhere, she would become a born-again Christian.

One day, I received the biggest surprise of my life after our 11:00 a.m. Sunday service. A young lady approached me and said, "That was a great message, Pastor Brian!"

"Oh, thank you!" I said, extending my hand to shake hers. "I'm Brian. Good to meet you."

She shook my hand and said, "I've met you before. A few times, actually."

I was confused. I tried to search my mental database for the faintest recollection of her, but I was drawing a complete blank.

"I'm sorry, remind me where we've met?"

She grinned.

"I came to your house years ago when you were discipling my boyfriend, and I attended a few of your services. I was the Wiccan who argued with you about God!"

"Oh, my goodness! Yes! How could I forget? I'm sorry I didn't recognize you."

Her beautiful smile only grew more radiant.

"I gave my life to Christ a few months ago and moved back to Minnesota to live with my parents."

"You're kidding me! How did that happen?"

"Well, I always remembered what you told me that night in your office the first time I met you. You know, how the Father loves us so much that He paid the ultimate sacrifice by sending His Son, Jesus, to die for us. I hated you for saying that, but your words haunted me for years. Eventually, I couldn't run from God anymore and gave my life to Jesus. I had to return to Albuquerque to thank you for sharing Jesus with me."

Come on! Only Jesus could write a script like that. And as it turns out, her ex-boyfriend is also serving Jesus today.

This is my point: Jesus loves people, and not a single person is beyond the reach of His grace—not even the person you think is utterly hopeless.

I didn't lead this young lady to faith in Jesus, but I prayed for her and planted seeds in her life that someone else watered, and many years later, they bore fruit.

The Apostle Paul wrote in 1 Corinthians 3:6-7: *"I planted the seed, Apollos watered it, but God has been making it grow. So neither the one who plants nor the one who waters is anything, but only God, who makes things grow."* To reap a harvest, you must plant seeds. Others might water them and even harvest the fruit of those seeds, but you must be faithful to plant them.

Keep loving people, praying for them, and sharing Jesus with them. It might seem like they aren't listening, but deep down, those seeds are taking root.

I hope this story encourages you to share Jesus with people even if you think there is *no way* they will ever turn to Jesus. Often we refrain from sharing the Gospel with people because we think they will reject it. But we must remember that sometimes, it's not about getting people to their final destination, but simply helping them start their journey toward God.

My friend Craig Groeschel, the pastor of Life.Church, once said, "You never know how God might use one conversation, one expression of love, or one moment of prayer to change someone's life."[67]

Share Jesus

The fifth habit in the B.L.E.S.S. strategy is to *share Jesus*. As you have been praying for people by name daily, listening to them, eating with them, and serving them, the Holy Spirit has undoubtedly been softening their hearts to receive the Gospel. Now it's time to share Jesus with them.

Be sensitive to the Spirit's leading. With Mazz, it took sixteen months before he was ready to hear the Gospel. Some people were ready the first day I met them, but it took years before others were open to hearing about Jesus. The Holy Spirit will guide you as you lean on Him.

A Passion for Souls

Do you want your life to count for eternity? Then focus on winning souls for Jesus. Proverbs 11:30 says, *"The fruit of the righteous is a tree of life, And he who wins souls is wise."*[68]

CHAPTER 7

King Edward VII invited William Booth, the founder of the Salvation Army, to Buckingham Palace in 1904. He wanted to honor him for his contributions to society. When the king asked Booth to sign his guest book, he wrote: "Some men's ambition is art. Some men's ambition is fame. Some men's ambition is gold. My ambition is the souls of men!"[69]

Paul was apprehended by this same passion for souls: *"I have great sorrow and unceasing anguish in my heart. For I could wish that I were cursed and cut off from Christ for the sake of my people, those of my own race"* (Romans 9:2-3). Paul's desire to see the Jewish people saved was so intense that he was even willing to go to hell if it meant they could be saved.

Today, as in the Book of Acts, God wants to instill a passion for souls in everyday believers. In the first century, ordinary believers spread the Gospel wherever they went, even under the threat of daily persecution (Acts 8:4).

Evangelism is not the job of *professionals*—full-time pastors and evangelists. It is the privilege and responsibility of every believer to share their faith. God wants to ignite your heart with the same passion for souls the early disciples had so you can see what they saw—entire cities and nations coming to Jesus.

God designed evangelism to be an overflow of our love for Jesus. The more we grow in our love for Jesus, the more we want to tell others about Him. We won't even need to try—it will be like a young woman who falls in love with a young man. She doesn't need to go through a four-week "falling in love class" to help her tell her friends and family about the love of her life. She won't shut up about him!

It's the same with Jesus. Peter and John said in Acts 4:20, *"As for us, we cannot help speaking about what we have seen and heard."* The apostles loved Jesus and couldn't stop talking about Him. Sharing Jesus was as natural to them as breathing. I want to invite you to fall in love with Jesus all over again or for the first time. As you do, evangelism won't feel like a burden or religious duty. It will naturally flow out of you because you will want everyone to know the same radical love that has transformed your life.

Everyone

"Jesus loves you and died for you." We hear those words so often that we can become desensitized to them. Our pastor says them every Sunday, and we think, "Yeah, yeah...I know that already. Can we move on to the other, more important stuff?"

But I'm going to ask you to pause and take a minute to meditate on this reality: Jesus loves you so much that He couldn't bear the thought of living without you for eternity. Your sins had separated you from God, and you could do nothing to balance the scales of morality. Death had its grip on you, and nothing could change your fate until Jesus said, "Kill Me instead."

Let that sink in.

Jesus exchanged His life for yours. And once you accept His grace and feel the weight of what He did for you, Jesus wants you to join His mission of sharing His love with those who don't know Him yet.

Do you know what kind of reaction Jesus' death and resurrection elicited from the disciples? Jesus commissioned His disciples in Mark 16:15, *"Go into all the world and preach the Good News to everyone,"* and that's precisely what they did. They went everywhere telling everyone about Jesus.

God is giving you and me the same charge. The Apostle Paul wrote in Romans 10:13-15: *"Everyone who calls on the name of the LORD will be saved." But how can they call on him to save them unless they believe in him? And how can they believe in him if they have never heard about him? And how can they hear about him unless someone tells them? And how will anyone go and tell them without being sent? That is why the Scriptures say, "How beautiful are the feet of messengers who bring good news!"*

Jesus loves everyone, and He wants everyone to be saved. John wrote in 1 John 2:2, *"He is the atoning sacrifice for our sins, and not only for ours but also for the sins of the whole world."* God is calling us to share the Gospel with *everyone* because Jesus died for *everyone.*

Jesus died for:

Every Jew and Gentile.

Every Muslim, Buddhist, Hindu, and Sikh.

Every Catholic, Evangelical, and Protestant.

Every Mormon, Agnostic, and non-religious person.

Every Scientologist. (I see you, Tom Cruise!)

Every Wiccan, New Ager, Atheist, and Satanist.

Every heterosexual, homosexual, and trans person.

Every conservative, liberal, and everyone in between.

Every rich, poor, and middle-class person.

Every man, woman, and child.

Jesus wants everyone to be part of His forever family. Our mission is to share the Gospel with everyone until the last person in the last village on the planet has heard about Jesus.

Now, not everyone *will* be saved. In God's sovereignty, He knows who will respond to grace and who will reject it. But He desires that everyone be saved, as Paul reinforced in 1 Timothy 2:3-4: *"God wants all people to be saved and to come to a knowledge of the truth."*

You might ask, "How can a God of love who died for everyone send people to hell?" That's a great question. The truth is God doesn't send people to hell—people send themselves to hell when they reject Jesus. Remember, God didn't create hell for people; He made it for the fallen angels. Jesus said in Matthew 25:41 that the eternal fire of hell was *"prepared for the devil and his angels."*

Paul and Barnabas said to the Jews in Pisidian Antioch in Acts 13:46, *"It was necessary that we first preach the word of God to you Jews. But since you have rejected it and judged yourselves unworthy of eternal life, we will offer it to the Gentiles."*[70] It wasn't God who rejected them or judged them unworthy of eternal life—that was their choice. Grace and eternal life were offered and rejected.

God wants everyone to spend eternity with Him and offers His grace to everyone. But He won't force people to follow Him; otherwise, they would be like robots. He wants people who will choose Him of their own free will. The great news is anyone can be saved if they turn to Jesus, even with their last breath. So don't lose hope for your loved ones.

We aren't sovereign and don't know who will respond to the Gospel. That is why we must cast a broad net over the whole of humanity—all eight billion souls and counting—so everyone can hear and respond. Jesus died for every person on the planet, not only for every ethnic group. And He is calling us to pray for everyone by name, listen to them, eat with them, serve them, and share Jesus with them.

Paul asks a fundamental question in Romans 10:14: *"How, then, can they call on the one they have not believed in? And how can they believe in the one of whom they have not heard? And how can they hear without someone preaching to them?"* People cannot call on the Lord unless they hear from you and me about Him. That's why we must tell everyone we know about Jesus.

Your mission on Earth is to share the Good News of Jesus with as many people as possible. Keeping the Gospel to yourself would be like if the world was dying of a painful, fatal disease, and you had the only cure but kept it a secret. People are dying without Jesus, but you can change that by sharing the Gospel with them.

Play the Whole Field

On March 22, 2023, in a match between Chile's top soccer teams, Cobresal and Colo-Colo, goalkeeper Leandro Requena set an unexpected world record. With thirteen minutes left on the clock and Cobresal already in the lead 2-0, Requena took what initially appeared to be an insignificant goal kick.

Colo-Colo goalkeeper, Brayan Cortés, was well outside his penalty area. As the ball soared, he saw the writing on the wall and sprinted back toward his goal. But he was too late. The ball landed with incredible momentum, bounced high over Cortés' head, and left him stranded in the middle of the field as it continued to roll toward the goal and past the goal line.

The crowd erupted into a frenzy, and Leandro Requena earned his place in history. According to TNT Sports Chile, the goal was scored from a distance of 101 meters. Once Guinness World Records ratify it, it will break the record for the longest-range goal in history.[71]

When sharing their faith, many believers feel like Leandro Requena as they try to score an already difficult goal alone with just one kick. I know I certainly did when I first began sharing my faith. My objective was to lead people to Christ in the first conversation, and if they didn't accept Christ, I felt like I had failed.

Often we think it's all on us to lead people to faith, but we forget God designed evangelism to be a *team* sport, not an *individual* sport. An end-to-end goalkeeper goal is one of the rarest events in soccer. It happens occasionally, but most soccer goals require teamwork and small incremental gains.

A left midfielder receives a pass, dribbles down the field a little before passing it back to the center, who then kicks it forward to a striker who dribbles it a little farther. He doesn't have a clear shot and passes it to the center forward, who finally takes the kick.

And guess what? He misses! The team has to regain the ball, and in the end, there may be multiple attempts and turnovers before they finally find the right opening and score.

In the same way, we must also learn to play the *whole field*. Don't become frustrated if you don't score a goal every time you share the Gospel. By all means, dribble in and take the kick if the conversation goes there. But if it doesn't, be okay with moving the ball forward a few yards or even inches by sharing the Gospel. Pray and believe God will send Kingdom teammates to share His love with that person at the right time.

If you don't score, it doesn't mean you have failed. In my experience, most people respond to Jesus after at least seven Gospel presentations. If you are the first person to share Jesus with someone, they likely won't accept Him on the spot. But don't be discouraged. God is pleased with you.

When fruit is ripe, it's easy to pluck from the tree. On the other hand, if it is unripe, it does not let go of its branch easily. And you may break the branch if you try to force it off.

Don't pressure people to accept Jesus. In doing so, you may inadvertently push them farther away from God. Let God continue to work in their lives until they are ready, and be grateful to be part of God's process, even if you aren't the one who walks them to the feet of Jesus. I didn't lead the Wiccan young lady to Jesus, but it brings me joy to know I shared in her salvation harvest.

And please don't misunderstand me: It is always the *right* time to share the Gospel. Every time you have a chance to share Jesus with someone—at the gym, in a restaurant, in the hotel elevator, at a coffee shop, or in the back seat of an Uber (I'm talking to you, Dave Gibson!)—go for it! But don't try to *force* people to accept Jesus. Trust that the Holy Spirit loves them more than you do. He is the one who will convict them and draw them to Jesus.

Jesus said in John 16:8, *"And when [the Holy Spirit] comes, he will convict the world of its sin, and of God's righteousness, and of the coming judgment."* Some Christians haven't received the memo that it's the Holy Spirit's job to convict the world of sin, not theirs.

It's not our responsibility to *convict* people—it's our duty to pray for them, love them, serve them, and share Jesus with them. You can *love* people into the Kingdom, but you can't *judge* them into the Kingdom. So let's leave the convicting to the Holy Spirit and focus on loving people.

Be Gentle and Respectful

The Apostle Peter gave us explicit instructions about how to share our faith in 1 Peter 3:15, *"But in your hearts revere Christ as Lord. Always be prepared to give an answer to everyone who asks you to give the reason for the hope that you have. But do this with gentleness and respect."*

Peter tells us to be ready to give an answer to everyone for the hope we have. As a Christian community, we've done a decent job at that. But way too often, we have totally missed the second half of this verse: "But do this with gentleness and respect."

Sadly, many Christians haven't been gentle or respectful toward people of other religions or those with no religious affiliation. Too often, we've been judgmental, harsh, and disrespectful, and we haven't won people to Jesus. I confess I was guilty of this for many years. If you want people to respect your faith, you must respect their faith. You might find that statement controversial, but I stand by it. The Bible says you reap what you sow. If you want to reap respect, you have to sow respect.

You don't need to agree with them or their beliefs to be respectful. That's not compromise—that's love, and love compels us to be respectful. Recording artist Aretha Franklin told the world what people want: "R-E-S-P-E-C-T: Find out what it means to me."[72]

And be *gentle*. Be kind, patient, and gentle instead of being mean, judgmental, and forceful. You will always catch more flies with honey than with vinegar. Don't pressure them or make them feel guilty. A little gentleness goes a long way in earning people's trust.

How to Share Your Faith

I want to give you a four-part strategy to share your faith and disciple people into a relationship with Jesus. It's simple, it's biblical, and it works.

1. Share your story.
Share the three parts of your story: before you met Jesus, how you met Jesus, and your life since you met Jesus.

2. Share God's story.

After you share your story, tell people about God's story, the Gospel.

3. Invite them to respond.

No Gospel presentation is complete without an invitation to respond to Jesus. If you don't ask them to respond, they probably won't.

4. Encourage them to take the next steps.

After people accept Jesus, encourage them to take the next steps to develop their relationship with Jesus. Help them grow spiritually.

1. Share Your Story

Paul said in Colossians 1:27, *"To them God has chosen to make known among the Gentiles the glorious riches of this mystery, which is Christ in you, the hope of glory."* The work of Christ inside you through the power of the Holy Spirit is the hope of glory. And it's the hope the world needs. They need the Jesus inside of you.

Our words and stories can't save people; only the Gospel can. But as we share the Gospel in the context of our story and tell people how Jesus has changed our lives, the Holy Spirit opens their hearts to Jesus. Personalize the Gospel by weaving God's story into your story. People need to hear your story because nobody else has your unique blend of experiences, hurts, and dreams.

Rick Warren explains the role of storytelling in the life of Jesus: "Jesus was the master storyteller. He'd say, 'Hey, did you hear the one about…' and then tell a parable to teach a truth. In fact, the Bible shows that storytelling was Jesus' favorite technique when speaking to the crowd: *'Jesus spoke all these things to the crowd in parables; he did not say anything to them without using a parable'* (Matthew 13:34). In fact, the entire Bible is essentially a book of God-inspired stories! That's how God has chosen to communicate His Word to human beings."[73]

Nobody told better stories than Jesus. People still remember His stories thousands of years later. Storytelling was the centerpiece of Jesus' communication style. Why? Because He created us with an innate need for story. The best way to teach truth is to embed it in a story. That's what the parables were—heavenly truths told through natural stories.

People crave good stories, funny stories, scary stories—because God hard-wired all of us to respond to stories. Jonathan Gottschall nailed it: "We are, as a species, addicted to story. Even when the body goes to sleep, the mind stays up all night, telling itself stories."[74]

Weaving God's story into your story can capture people's attention like nothing else. When the Apostle Paul shared the Gospel with a hostile crowd in Acts 22, he shared it through his personal story.

He shared his experiences in three sections: his life before Jesus, how he met Jesus, and his life after Jesus. I want to show you, from Paul's example, how to share the Gospel using the three parts of your story:

A. Your life before Jesus.
B. How you met Jesus.
C. Your life since you met Jesus.

(A) Your life before Jesus

"'Brothers and fathers, listen now to my defense.' When they heard him speak to them in Aramaic, they became very quiet. Then Paul said: 'I am a Jew, born in Tarsus of Cilicia, but brought up in this city. I studied under Gamaliel and was thoroughly trained in the law of our ancestors. I was just as zealous for God as any of you are today.

"'I persecuted the followers of this Way to their death, arresting both men and women and throwing them into prison, as the high priest and all the Council can themselves testify. I even obtained letters from them to their associates in Damascus, and went there to bring these people as prisoners to Jerusalem to be punished.'" — Acts 22:1-5

Paul shared the first part of his story—what he was like before he met Jesus. He was a devout Jew who studied under Gamaliel, one of the most respected doctors of Jewish law. Paul saw Christianity as an existential threat to Judaism and was committed to extinguishing every vestige of this new faith. He even had many Christians arrested and killed. Now let's talk about you.

What was your life like before Jesus?

Were you an alcoholic or a drug addict?

Were you a businessman who neglected his family?

Were you an abusive father or an absent mother?

Were you a morally good person who did not feel the need for a Savior?

Were you a member of a gang or incarcerated?

Were you a troubled child who couldn't cope with your parents' divorce?

Were you a military veteran struggling with PTSD?

CHAPTER 7

Were you sexually active, going from partner to partner? Were you a lonely teenager watching others live their lives on social media, dreaming of a better life?

Were you someone who simply had never heard much about Jesus?

Whether you come from a past of regret, pain, pride, or emptiness, it is important to share where Jesus found you because chances are your hearers can relate to your story in more ways than one and realize their need for a Savior.

(B) How you met Jesus

"About noon as I came near Damascus, suddenly a bright light from heaven flashed around me. I fell to the ground and heard a voice say to me, 'Saul! Saul! Why do you persecute me?' 'Who are you, Lord?' I asked.

'I am Jesus of Nazareth, whom you are persecuting,' he replied. My companions saw the light, but they did not understand the voice of him who was speaking to me. 'What shall I do, Lord?' I asked. 'Get up,' the Lord said, 'and go into Damascus. There you will be told all that you have been assigned to do.' My companions led me by the hand into Damascus, because the brilliance of the light had blinded me." — Acts 22:6-11

Immediately after telling his audience who he was before, Paul explains how he met Jesus and surrendered his life to Him. He vividly describes his encounter with Jesus to paint a picture in his listeners' minds. Before I continue, let me tell you something. Paul's story is not more powerful than yours. Rick Warren says: "There is only one way to God: through

128

His Son, Jesus. He is the only way to the Father. But there are a thousand ways to Jesus."

What were the circumstances that led you to Jesus?

Did you meet Jesus at a vacation Bible school or a summer youth camp?

Sitting inside a jail cell?

At a college pizza party where a radical Jesus follower shared God's love with you?

Did you flip through the channels on your television and land on a Billy Graham crusade broadcast?

At your grandmother's funeral, grieving her loss?

Over coffee with a friend?

After being dragged by your neighbor to church?

Talking to a stranger on an airplane?

In the line of the soup kitchen with your three children?

In the chapel of a drug addiction recovery home?

At a youth group you only attended so you could hang out with a pretty girl?

Maybe you were raised in a Christian home and have believed in Jesus for as long as you remember. Perhaps you've heard the radical testimonies of people who were drug traffickers or strip club performers, and you think, "Compared to them, I don't have a story to tell!"

Nothing could be farther from the truth. You may have the greatest story of all. Your story is proof that God's transformative work is *real.* You are the living embodiment of what God can do across generations. Perhaps, as with my friend, Holden, your story is about growing up in a Christian family and attending church your whole life. But you had to discover your own personal relationship with Jesus.

Holden puts it this way: "I was born into a Christian family, and I accepted Jesus into my life when I was a kid. But I didn't fully surrender my life to Jesus until I was eighteen." Never dismiss your story—it has the potential to impact millions of people who can relate to your journey.

(C) Your life since you met Jesus

"A man named Ananias came to see me. He was a devout observer of the law and highly respected by all the Jews living there. He stood beside me and said, 'Brother Saul, receive your sight!' And at that very moment I was able to see him.

"Then he [Ananias] said: 'The God of our ancestors has chosen you to know his will and to see the Righteous One and to hear words from his mouth. You will be his witness to all people of what you have seen and heard. And now, what are you waiting for? Get up, be baptized, and wash your sins away, calling on his name.' When I returned to Jerusalem and was praying at the temple, I fell into a trance and saw the Lord speaking to me. 'Quick!' he said.

"'Leave Jerusalem immediately, because the people here will not accept your testimony about me.' 'Lord,' I replied, 'these people know that I went from one synagogue to another to imprison and beat those who believe in you.

"And when the blood of your martyr Stephen was shed, I stood there giving my approval and guarding the clothes of those who were killing him.' Then the Lord said to me, 'Go; I will send you far away to the Gentiles.'" — Acts 22:12-21

As Paul lays out his story, he shares the most riveting part—what happened to him after he accepted Jesus Christ as his Lord and Savior. The third element in your story is to tell people what happened to you after you met Jesus.

What has happened since you met Jesus?

How has your life changed?

Did your relationships improve?

Were you better equipped to handle your rage and anger?

Was the empty void in your heart filled?

Were you finally able to conquer that secret struggle?

Did you get better at dealing with your addictions?

What happened to your marriage?

Could your co-workers tell that you were different?

Were you able to give more love to your children?

Did you discover a new joy and peace?

Did the grip money had on you lift?

Were you finally able to lift your hands in worship?

Did you discover a new purpose in Christ?

2. Share God's Story

The second part of sharing your faith with people is introducing them to God's story, the Gospel. Paul said in Romans 1:16: *"For I am not ashamed of the gospel, because it is the power of God that brings salvation to everyone who believes: first to the Jew, then to the Gentile."*

What is the Gospel? The word *Gospel* simply means "good news." The Gospel isn't merely a message to save unbelievers; it is the foundation of our Christian life.

Let me share the Gospel of Jesus Christ with you as simply as possible.

God created you in His image, loves you unconditionally, and longs to have a personal relationship with you. But the problem is your sin has separated you from a holy God. That is why God sent His Son, Jesus, to take the punishment for your sins.

Jesus was born of the Virgin Mary, lived a sinless life, died on the cross, rose from the dead three days later, and is now seated at the right hand of the Father in heaven. Jesus is the only way to heaven because He was the only sinless sacrifice that could atone for our sins and appease the wrath of God.

So, how can you be saved? The Bible says in Ephesians 2:8 that we are "saved by grace through faith." Grace means unmerited favor. God is offering you a new life and a fresh start, even though you don't deserve it. You will never be good enough to earn salvation or be bad enough to be disqualified. Since Jesus paid the price for our sins, He has the right to decide how we receive His gift.

There are two steps in the process of salvation:

1. Believe in Jesus. Put your faith in Jesus alone for your salvation and confess that Jesus is Lord. Romans 10:9 says, *"If you confess with your mouth, 'Jesus is Lord,' and believe in your heart that God raised him from the dead, you will be saved."*

The Philippian jailor asked Paul and Silas, *"What must I do to be saved?"* They replied, *"Believe in the Lord Jesus and you will be saved, you and your whole household."* (Acts 16:31)

If you will believe in Jesus and put your trust in Him for salvation, He will give you *saving* faith—not only for you, but faith for your whole family to be saved. Even the ability to believe in Jesus is a response to God's grace. No person can take credit for their salvation—it's all grace from start to finish.

As you share the Gospel with people, focus more on what Christ has already done for them—His finished work of grace on the cross—than on what they need to do. Jesus said it more clearly than anyone else in human history in John 3:16 when he told Nicodemus, *"For God so loved the world that he gave his one and only Son, that whoever believes in him shall not perish but have eternal life."* Believe in Jesus and receive His free gift of salvation.

2. Repent of your sins. As you believe in God, He will give you the desire and grace to repent. Repentance means a change of mind that leads to a changed life. As you begin to think differently, you will begin to act differently. You will begin to hate sin and love righteousness because God's Spirit inside you is giving you the desire to be like Jesus.

Acts 11:18 says, *"So then, even to the Gentile God has granted repentance that leads to life."* Notice that it is God who *grants* repentance to people. Unbelievers are incapable of "turning from their sins" by themselves—they need God's help. But once God grants them repentance in response to a believing heart, the Holy Spirit begins to transform them from the inside out.

A changed life flows out of a changed heart and mind, and only faith in Christ can change a sinner—it's not the result of human effort (Ephesians 2:1-10).

God will give you the grace to turn away from sin, and turn to God with all your heart. Peter said in Acts 3:19: *"Repent, then, and turn to God, so that your sins may be wiped out, that times of refreshing may come from the Lord."*

One of my best friends, Greg Stier, the founder and visionary of Dare 2 Share, uses the acronym G.O.S.P.E.L. to explain the core message of the Gospel. I have memorized it, and I would encourage you to do so, as well:

GOD created us to be with Him.
OUR sins separate us from God.
SINS cannot be removed by good deeds.
PAYING the price for sin, Jesus died and rose again.
EVERYONE who trusts in Him alone has eternal life.
LIFE with Jesus starts now and lasts forever!

Greg has graciously written a brief training to help you share the Gospel. This training can be found in the Appendix. Please read it and use it. (Thanks, Greg! You're a real champion!)

I have shared the Gospel thousands of times. When I do, I share the same core Gospel truths and Bible verses nearly every time because the core message of the Gospel never changes. Still, I've never shared the Gospel the same *way* twice.

That's because every time I have shared the Gospel, I was different from the last time I shared it, and the people I was sharing it with were different. Maybe they only need one Bible verse, or they might need to read the Gospel of John with you before they will believe. Everyone is different.

Paul said in Romans 8:14, *"For those who are led by the Spirit of God are the children of God."* Allow the Holy Spirit to lead you because He knows what people need and what you can say that will impact them.

My advice is this: Don't feel compelled to follow a script. Embrace the Holy Spirit. Be fully present in the moment and allow the Spirit to deliver a message perfectly tailored to the person or people you are sharing with.

3. Invite Them to Respond

After you share your story and the Gospel with people, be bold and invite them to respond. Often people are convicted and want to embrace Christ, but nobody gives them an opportunity to do so. Ask them, "How do you feel about what I just shared? Do you have any questions?" If they have questions, try to answer them, trusting the Holy Spirit to help you. And don't worry about knowing the answers to all their questions.

If they don't have any questions, ask them, "Do you want to put your faith in Jesus now?" or "Do you want to accept Jesus as your Lord and Savior?" If they say "yes," lead them in a simple prayer of repentance.

While it's true that "the sinner's prayer" is not in the Bible, I have found that leading people in a simple prayer helps them seal their decision to follow Jesus. Of course, it's not the prayer that saves them—Jesus saves them as a response to their repentance and faith.

I often lead people in a prayer similar to this, asking them to repeat after me:

"Jesus, I believe You are the Son of God. I believe You died on the cross for my sins. But three days later, You rose from the dead and became the Savior of the world. Today I confess my sins to You. Please forgive me, change me, and give me a new life. I confess You are my Lord and my Savior. Come into my heart and change my life. In Jesus' name, I pray."

On the other hand, if they say "no," to taking the next step, invite them to continue meeting with you to explore Christianity. If they don't want to discuss Jesus anymore, respect their wishes (unless Jesus tells you otherwise). Focus on building your relationship with them.

4. Encourage Them to Take the Next Steps

Now the fun begins! If you lead someone to Jesus, don't leave them hanging—celebrate with them and help them start this new chapter of their life. Encourage them to take the next steps to grow in their relationship with God.

This is a very important time in their walk with God. Think back to the time when you received Jesus as your Lord and Savior. When I came to Jesus, I was overwhelmed by His love. I was hungry and wanted to learn as much as possible about God and the Bible.

It's what the Bible calls "our first love." Most new believers go through this "honeymoon" phase when they meet Jesus. They want more and more of Jesus, and it is the best time to instill habits in them that will satisfy their present hunger and sustain them as they grow in their faith.

A. Start Reading the Bible Daily. The Gospel of John is a great place to start. Offer to read through the Bible with them. Help them download the Bible app on their phones. YouVersion.com. They can listen to God's Word on the Bible app if they dislike reading.

B. Pray daily. Pray out loud with them so they can learn how to pray. Tell them to talk to Jesus as they would talk to a friend and to carve out time every day to pray.

C. Be Water-Baptized. Encourage them to be water baptized as a public confession of their faith in Jesus. In the Bible, most people were water baptized immediately after they got saved.

D. Join a Community. Encourage them to join a small group and attend church with you. They need a Christian community where they can grow spiritually.

E. Share Your Faith. After Andrew encountered Jesus, he went home and told his brother Peter about Him. You are the most contagious right after you get infected. Don't wait to share your faith until you have it all figured out. Start telling everyone about what Jesus has done in your life.

Put It into Practice

The brother of Jesus said in James 1:22, "But don't just listen to God's Word. You must do what it says. Otherwise, you are only fooling yourselves."[75] The Bible will only work for you if you put it into practice. I encourage you to take about thirty minutes to reflect and write the three parts of your story, your Gospel presentation, and a sample invitation for people to respond to Jesus. Write as if you were talking to a friend. This will help prepare you to share it with others.

CHAPTER 7

A

My Story

1. My life before I met Jesus:

2. How I met Jesus:

3. My life since I met Jesus:

By **NAME**

B

God's Story

Summarize the Gospel in your own words.

C

The Invitation

Invite them to accept Jesus or to continue the conversation the next time you meet, depending on their response.

139

Call to Action

Now that you have written the three parts to your story, a personal Gospel presentation, and an invitation to confess Jesus or explore Christianity further, I want to encourage you to take two more bold steps of faith.

First, practice your story with at least two followers of Jesus. Practice makes perfect; at least, that's what my college guitar teacher told me. (Still waiting for that one to come true thirty-one years later!)

Second, after a few practice runs, go for the real thing. Share Jesus with one of the five people you have been praying for daily. Just relax and be *yourself*—everybody else is already taken! People are attracted to authenticity, so just be you. Rely on the Holy Spirit to give you the words to share. Take a step of faith and share with someone.

Chapter 7: Takeaways

 KEY POINTS:

- Evangelism is not the job of *professionals*. It is the privilege and responsibility of every believer.
- God designed evangelism to be an overflow of our love for Jesus. The more we grow in our love for Jesus, the more we want to tell others about Him.
- God is calling us to share the Gospel with *everyone* because Jesus died for *everyone*.
- It is always the *right* time to share the Gospel.
- People crave good stories, funny stories, scary stories—because God hard-wired all of us to respond to stories.
- There is a four-part strategy to share your faith and disciple people into a relationship with Jesus:
  1. Share your story: Before you met Jesus, how you met Jesus, and your life since you met Jesus.
  2. Share God's story: Share the Gospel with them.
  3. Invite them to respond to the Gospel.
  4. Encourage them to take the next steps in their walk with God: Read the Bible, pray daily, be water-baptized, join a community, and share their faith.

 MEMORY VERSE:

1 Peter 3:15: *"But in your hearts revere Christ as Lord. Always be prepared to give an answer to everyone who asks you to give the reason for the hope that you have. But do this with gentleness and respect."*

A PRAYER:

Jesus, thank You for dying for the sins of the whole world and for inviting me to partner with You in saving souls. Lord, give me a burden for people far from God. Create opportunities for me to share the Gospel with the five people I am praying for daily. Lord, soften their hearts to receive Jesus and soften mine to always be ready to tell them about You.

 SELF-REFLECTION QUESTIONS:

1. 1. When was the last time you shared the Gospel with someone?
2. 2. If you have not shared your faith yet, what has kept you from doing so?
3. 3. After reading this chapter, how would you share your story (testimony) with others?
4. 4. Some people are afraid to share the Gospel because they do not know how to explain it. Have you taken the time to understand and practice explaining the Gospel?

 CALL TO ACTION:

1. Practice your story with at least two followers of Jesus.
2. Share Jesus with one of the five people you have been praying for daily. Rely on the Holy Spirit to give you the right words to share.

CHAPTER 8

CALL TO ACTION

Billions of people around the world don't know Jesus, but God has given you and me the power to change that. And it all starts with prayer. Prayer is the catalyst—the fire that ignites your heart for God's mission.

God is asking you the same question He asked the prophet in Isaiah 6:8, "Whom shall I send?" Will you answer and say: "Here am I, send me" to my friends, family, neighbors, and co-workers?

Have you ever seen a person drive to a gas station, fill up with premium fuel, and then leave his car there? No, after we fill our cars with fuel, we get into our cars, and go where the fuel can take us. In the same way, this book is fuel for what comes next. And I've got good news for you: You're what's next!

It's your turn to take what you've learned in this book and apply it in your home, your neighborhood, your school, your workplace, your church, your denomination, and everywhere your love for souls will take you.

Whether you're a believer determined to see your loved ones come to Jesus or a church leader wanting to engage believers in prayer and evangelism, there are several ways to activate what you have learned.

CHAPTER 8

Believers

1. BLESS 5: Start praying daily for five people far from God and share Jesus with them using the B.L.E.S.S. lifestyle—pray for them, listen to them, eat with them, serve them, and share Jesus with them. Complete the B.L.E.S.S. card after this chapter.

2. JOIN A GLOBAL COMMUNITY: We would love for you to join a global community of Christ-followers who are using the B.L.E.S.S. practices to pray for people and share their faith. When you sign up, you will receive reminders and exclusive content to help you live out a B.L.E.S.S. lifestyle.

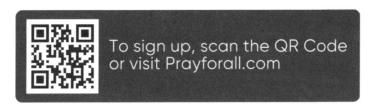

To sign up, scan the QR Code or visit Prayforall.com

Church & Ministry Leaders

If you lead a church, ministry, or business and want to partner with us, visit our website prayforall.com. Click on Partner With Us and sign up to receive access to all our free implementation resources for organizations.

To partner with us, scan the QR Code or visit Prayforall.com/partners

Once you have the resources you need, implement the Pray for All Initiative in your organization using our Implementation Strategy.

pray for all

IMPLEMENTATION STRATEGY

Here are seven steps to implementing
the Pray for All Initiative in your context:

① COMMIT TO IT:

Whether you lead a church, a network, or a denomination, commit to making the B.L.E.S.S. lifestyle the norm in your own life and in your church or ministry for years to come. Don't teach on the B.L.E.S.S. lifestyle until you're living it out yourself. Pray for 5 people far from God and seek every opportunity to bless them.

Then share it with your leadership team and invite them to join you in blessing others. The B.L.E.S.S. Lifestyle will take root in your church if its pastors and leaders put it into practice and lead by example.

Scan the code to have access to all of our free resources.

② EMPOWER & EQUIP:

Empower a capable leader who can review our resources and equip your team to implement this initiative in their department.

We have designed step-by-step guides and resources he/she can share with your ministry teams.

Implementation Guides

Presentation Resources

Print-Ready Resources

Small Group Resources

Youth Ministry Resources

Kids Ministry Resources

③ LAUNCH IT:

Choose a date and time to launch Pray for All at your church. When the date comes, create a festive environment and share the vision of praying for loved ones and sharing Jesus with them. Ask everyone to write down the names of 5 people they will pray for by name.

Launch Pray for All with a **BLESS 5 Campaign**, so your members get to practice the 5 B.L.E.S.S. habits for 5 weeks:

- *Begin with prayer*
- *Listen to them*
- *Eat with them*
- *Serve them*
- *Share Jesus with them*

Scan the code to download helpful tips for your BLESS 5 Campaign Launch.

④ NURTURE IT:

During those five weeks, teach on the B.L.E.S.S. lifestyle to keep it front and center in people's minds:

- *Teach it on Sundays*
- *Teach it in small groups,*
- *Make it a part of new member classes*
- *Incorporate it into your discipleship*
- *tracks, kids' ministry, and student ministry.*

To learn more about the B.L.E.S.S. Lifestyle, you can read Brian Alarid's book, 'By Name.'

⑤ CELEBRATE IT:

End the five weeks with a service/event to which all who were prayed for are invited and get to hear the Gospel. Recognize people privately and publicly for praying, listening, eating, serving, and sharing Jesus with others. Celebrate testimonies of changed lives.

We would love to hear what God does in your church. Scan the QR code to share your story with us.

⑥ REPEAT IT:

Once the campaign is over, continue to take a few minutes every Sunday to pray for people far from God. We recommend churches do BLESS 5 campaigns 3-4 times a year. Make this strategy part of your church culture until everyone is won for Jesus.

As your members witness salvations and life-change in their 5, encourage them to continue adding new people to their prayer list.

B.L.E.S.S. *Card*

PRAY *for* 5

TAKE 5 MINUTES A DAY TO
PRAY FOR 5
PEOPLE BY NAME
WHO NEED JESUS

1. _____
2. _____
3. _____
4. _____
5. _____

Ways to PRAY

1. Father, draw them to your Son Jesus (John 6:44).
2. Father, remove their spiritual blindness so they will believe the Gospel (2 Cor. 4:4; Acts 16:14).
3. Father, give them the gift of repentance to turn from their sins (John 16:8; 2 Tim. 2:25-26).
4. Father, give me opportunities and boldness to share the Gospel with them (Col. 4:3-4; Acts 4:29-31).
5. Father, please save them and their whole family (Acts 16:31).

SHARE JESUS WITH THEM BY LIVING OUT
The **B.L.E.S.S.** *Lifestyle*
Begin with prayer | Listen to them | Eat with Them
Serve Them | Share Jesus with Them

APPENDIX: THE GOSPEL

BY GREG STIER

How do you share the Gospel message in a simple way, from takeoff to touchdown?

Sharing the Gospel is like flying a plane. First of all, you must get fueled up by the right motivation (love for the Lord, compassion for the lost, urgency of the mission, etc.). Making sure we are fueled by the right motivation is important. Sharing the Gospel is not just to check it off your spiritual checklist, but should flow out of love for God to others.

After you get fueled up with the right motivation, you need to get passengers on board. How do you do that? You pray for them, care for them, and then look for that natural opportunity to share the Gospel with them (aloud with words).

But what do you say when that opportunity arises? How do you even bring it up? If someone says, "It's hot in here," do you say, "It's hot in hell, let me tell you about it!"

No, of course not.

When God opens this door, you want to have a natural Gospel conversation, not just an evangelistic presentation.

This is when you learn how to "take off" and begin down the runway of sharing your faith. To do that, I encourage you to learn how to "Ask, Admire, and Admit."

Ask good questions. Get to know them personally. When the time is right, ask a spiritual question like, "How can I pray for you?" or "Do you have any spiritual beliefs?" or "Do you go to church anywhere?"

Admire where they are at spiritually. Like Paul in Acts 17, who admired that the pagan philosophers of Athens were "very religious," find at least one area of their belief system you can admire. You may not agree with everything, but there's probably something you can admire (i.e., a Muslim's commitment to prayer, a Hindu's belief in the supernatural, an atheist's commitment to science and reason, etc.).

This admiration begins to bring the walls down and helps you "engage, not enrage" the person you are talking to about spiritual things.

After you have "admired," it's now time to "admit." This is when you let that person know how much you personally need Jesus. This is when you tell the story of how Jesus saved you from your sin and from a wasted life.

By now you are flying and having a Gospel conversation.

Now's the time to take them through your flight plan. This is the Gospel message. At Dare 2 Share we use a G.O.S.P.E.L. acrostic that clearly explains the whole story of the Gospel from Genesis 1-Revelation 22 and truly helps guide you through the core message of the Good News of Jesus.

God created us to be with Him	Genesis 1-2
Our sins separate us from God	Genesis 3
Sins cannot be removed by good deeds	Gen. 4, Mal. 4
Paying the price for sin, Jesus died and rose again	Matt., Luke
Everyone who trusts in Him alone has eternal life	John
Life with Jesus starts now and lasts forever	Acts, Rev.

It's important to navigate someone through the whole story of the Gospel. That's the power of this acrostic. It tells the whole story.

It starts in the Garden of Eden with Adam, Eve, and their Creator. Everything was good. God made the first man and woman in His image and for His glory. They were in perfect relationship with Him and each other (Psalm 100:3).

Then sin entered the picture and ruined everything. Adam and Eve broke God's command and God's heart. They were kicked out of the presence of this holy God and, as a result, all of humanity was sentenced to suffer God's wrath forever (Romans 3:23; 6:23).

No amount of good deeds could ever remove the stain of this sin from the human heart. Good deeds and religious acts just cover over our sin, they can't cleanse us from them (Isaiah 64:6).

So, 2,000 years ago, God sent His one and only Son to became one of us. Jesus, fully God and fully human, fully paid the price for our sins with His own death on the cross (Romans 5:8).

Three days later Jesus rose from the dead and offers eternal life to all those who simply trust in Him alone to forgive them from their sins and give them eternal life (John 3:16). This life is a personal relationship with God that begins at the moment of salvation and stretches into eternity (John 17:3).

Master the acrostic, like a pilot masters the instruments in the cockpit, and you'll be able to clearly share the Gospel story.

Sometimes when flying, you encounter turbulence. As you take your friend through the Gospel flight plan, sometimes they'll want to argue or have a question that you don't have the answer to.

APPENDIX

Pray, be calm, and just say, "I don't know, but I'll try to find the answer this week," and then go find it (scour your Bible, ask your pastor, etc.) so that you can continue the conversation.

How do you "land the plane" when it comes to evangelism?

Ask two questions after you've explained the Gospel:

Does that make sense?

Is there anything holding you back from trusting in Jesus right now?

If it doesn't make sense or if there is something holding them back, do your best to help re-explain the Gospel and deal with their objections. Don't force them to believe. Remember the Spirit of God must open their eyes.

But if they are ready, challenge them to trust in Jesus on the spot, lead them in a prayer of thanksgiving, get them involved in a church, and challenge them to share the good news with someone else.

This is how you share the Gospel from "take off to touch down."

An easy way to share the Gospel using "automatic pilot" is to download the free *Life in 6 Words* app. It infuses all of these principles into a simple faith sharing app.

Tools & Resources

The Pray for All Strategy is simple and can be implemented with or without technology. For churches whose members have easy access to the internet, we offer apps and digital tools. For churches whose members cannot depend on digital resources and technology, we have designed tools that can be easily printed out and used in their context.

Scan de QR Code or visit PrayForAll.com/Resources to view the many resources we offer.

IMPLEMENTATION
Resources

PRESENTATION
Resources

PRINTING
Resources

MULTIMEDIA
Resources

SOCIAL MEDIA
Resources

CHILDREN'S
Resources

YOUTH
Resources

SMALL GROUP
Resources

Print-Ready Resources

Free Online Course

By Name

MyJourney

HOW TO PRAY FOR PEOPLE AND LEAD THEM TO JESUS

READY TO START?

ENROLL IN THIS FREE ONLINE COURSE

155

ABOUT THE AUTHOR

Brian Alarid is the president and founder of America Prays and World Prays and the chairman of Pray For All. He is the author of two books: *When People Pray: What Happens When Ordinary People Pray to an Extraordinary God* and *By Name: How to Pray for People and Lead Them to Jesus*.

Brian has more than thirty years of experience in pastoral ministry and executive leadership. He has equipped and inspired thousands of people all around the world through conferences, crusades, television, and radio.

Brian has a master's degree in organizational leadership from Regent University. He has been married to Mercy Alarid for twenty-six years. They reside in Guatemala City with their three children.

I would love to hear from you!

Email: brian@brianalarid.com
Websites: BrianAlarid.com | ByNameBook.com
Twitter: @BrianAlarid
Facebook: Brian Alarid Ministries
Instagram: @BrianAlarid
LinkedIn: Linkedin.com/in/BrianAlarid

Scan the QR Code or go to https://wkf.ms/3nopdZP to request Brian to speak at your event.

ENDNOTES

1. Isaiah 43:1, English Standard Version

2. Marable, Manning, et al. Let Nobody Turn Us Around: Voices of Resistance, Reform and Renewal: An African American Anthology. Edited by Leith Mullings. Bowker, 2000.

3. "What About Bob? (1991) - IMDb." IMDb, www.imdb.com/title/tt0103241/quotes/qt5644443. Accessed 10 Mar. 2023.

4. "About Us – Empowered21." About Us – Empowered21, empowered21.com/about. Accessed 11 Mar. 2023.

5. "A Goal Is a Dream With a Deadline - Business Fitness." Business Fitness, businessfitness.biz/a-goal-is-a-dream-with-a-deadline. Accessed 9 Mar. 2023

6. Victor Hugo - Wikiquote, en.wikiquote.org/wiki/Victor_Hugo. Accessed 9 Mar. 2023.

7. "It Always Seems Impossible Until It's Done." News, 29 July 2016, www.news.com.au/technology/innovation/inventions/the-life-changing-inventions-the-experts-said-were-impossible/news-story/8c-8b0e58532b329d1b6f97c3dfee9fcc. Accessed 3 Feb. 2023.

8. Turner, By Ash, and https://www.bankmycell.com/. "3.12 Billion More Phones Than People in the World!" BankMyCell, 10 July 2018, www.bankmycell.com/blog/how-many-phones-are-in-the-world.

9. "It Always Seems Impossible Until It's Done." News, 29 July 2016, www.news.com.au/technology/innovation/inventions/the-life-changing-inventions-the-experts-said-were-impossible/news-story/8c-8b0e58532b329d1b6f97c3dfee9fcc. Accessed 3 Feb. 2023.

10. https://financesonline.com/number-of-flights-worldwide. Accessed 3 Feb. 2023.

11. "It Always Seems Impossible Until It's Done." News, 29 July 2016, www.news.com.au/technology/innovation/inventions/the-life-

changing-inventions-the-experts-said-were-impossible/news-story/8c-8b0e58532b329d1b6f97c3dfee9fcc. Accessed 3 Feb. 2023.

12.   Ibid.

13.   Loisy, Nicolas de. "How Many Computers Are There in the World? &Mdash; SCMO." SCMO, 9 Aug. 2019, www.scmo.net/faq/2019/8/9/how-many-compaters-is-there-in-the-world.

14.   Roger Bannister: First Sub-four-minute Mile." Guinness World Records, www.guinnessworldrecords.com/records/hall-of-fame/first-sub-four-minute-mile. Accessed 11 Mar. 2023.

15.   "Quote by Muhammad Ali: "Impossible Is Just a Big Word Thrown Around By ...," www.goodreads.com/quotes/121663-impossi-ble-is-just-a-big-word-thrown-around-by-small. Accessed 9 Mar. 2023.

16.   Michelangelo - Wikiquote, https://en.wikiquote.org/wiki/Michelangelo. Accessed 9 Mar. 2023.

17.   Coelho, Paulo. The Alchemist. HarperOne, 2015.

18.   Coalition, Alexa. "Alexa Coalition." Alexa Coalition, alexacoalition.org/the-significance-of-names. Accessed 9 Mar. 2023.

19.   Shakespeare, William, 1564-1616. Romeo and Juliet, 1597. Oxford :published for the Malone Society by Oxford University Press, 2000.

20.   "Ice, ice, baby." https://genius.com/Vanilla-ice-ice-ice-baby-lyrics. Accessed 15 Mar. 2023.

21.   Coalition, Alexa. "Alexa Coalition." Alexa Coalition, alexacoalition.org/the-significance-of-names. Accessed 9 Mar. 2023.

22.   1 Timothy 2:1 Lexicon: First of All, Then, I Urge That Entreaties and Prayers, Petitions and Thanksgivings, Be Made on Behalf of All Men, biblehub.com/lexicon/1_timothy/2-1.htm. Accessed 9 Mar. 2023.

23.   Sinek, Simon. Start With Why: How Great Leaders Inspire Everyone to Take Action. Portfolio, 2010.

24.   Eastman, Dick. Love on Its Knees: Make a Difference by Praying for Others. 1989.

25. Ibid.

26. Revelation 2:17, New Living Translation

27. "Astro for Kids: How Many Stars Are There in Space?" Astronomy.com, astronomy.com/news/astro-for-kids/2021/09/astro-for-kids-how-many-stars-are-there-in-space. Accessed 9 Mar. 2023.

28. Hildebrant, Kyle. "Why We Name: The Power of Taming to Drive Deep Connections With a Brand." OVO, 24 July 2019, brandsbyovo.com/why-we-name-drive-connections-with-brand. Accessed 8 Mar. 2023.

29. Isaiah 49:16, New Living Translation

30. Isaiah 43:1, English Standard Version

31. Osteen, Joel. The Power of I Am: Two Words That Will Change Your Life Today. Faithwords, 2015.

32. Lucado, Max. When God Whispers Your Name. Bowker, 1998.

33. "I Have Called You By Name." The Chosen, created by Dallas Jenkins, season 1, episode 1, Angel Studios, 2019.

34. Svoboda, Martin. "There Isn't Time--so Brief Is Life--for Bickerings,...." Quotepark.com, quotepark.com/quotes/1149378-mark-twain-there-isnt-time-so-brief-is-life-for-bickerings. Accessed 10 Mar. 2023.

35. Guterson, David. Snow Falling on Cedars. Harcourt Brace & Company, 1994.

36. Ferguson, Dave, and Jon Ferguson. Bless: 5 Everyday Ways to Love Your Neighbor and Change the World. 2021.

37. Library, Billy Graham. "The Power of Prayer - the Billy Graham Library Blog." The Billy Graham Library, 1 Jan. 2014, billygrahamlibrary.org/the-power-of-prayer. Accessed 8 Mar. 2023.

38. "The Spurgeon Center." The Spurgeon Center, 1 Jan. 1869, www.spurgeon.org/resource-library/sermons/soul-winning. Accessed 11 Mar. 2023.

39. "Category: Evangelism." GeorgeMuller.org, 8 June 2017, https://

www.georgemuller.org/quotes/category/evangelism. Accessed 7 Mar. 2023.

40.   Arias, David. "St. Augustine: The Son Of Such Tears - Spiritual-Direction.com." SpiritualDirection.com, 27 Aug. 2020, spiritualdirection.com/2020/08/27/63597. Accessed 11 Mar. 2023.

41.   Tony Robbins In LinkedIn: It's Not What We Do Once in a While That Shapes Our Lives. It's What We Do… | 229 Comentarios, cl.linkedin.com/posts/officialtonyrobbins_its-not-what-we-do-once-in-a-while-that-activity-6964959172232716288-fS0t. Accessed 10 Mar. 2023.

42.   2 Timothy 1:3, New Living Translation.

43.   "Karl a. Menninger Quotes." BrainyQuote, www.brainyquote.com/quotes/karl_a_menninger_143978. Accessed 10 Mar. 2023.

44.   Nichols, Ralph. Are You Listening? The science of improving your listening ability for a better understanding of people. McGraw-Hill Companies, 1967.

45.   "Listening as Spiritual Hospitality - Henri Nouwen." Henri Nouwen, henrinouwen.org/meditations/listening-spiritual-hospitality. Accessed 10 Mar. 2023.

46.   "The Critical Role of Listening in the Communication Process." ThoughtCo, 6 Jan. 2019, www.thoughtco.com/listening-communication-term-1691247.

47.   Proverbs 20:12, New Living Translation

48.   "What Great Listeners Actually Do." Harvard Business Review, 14 July 2016, hbr.org/2016/07/what-great-listeners-actually-do.

49.   Ibid.

50.   Spence, Jacq. "Nonverbal Communication: How Body Language and Nonverbal Cues Are Key." Lifesize, 18 Feb. 2020, www.lifesize.com/blog/speaking-without-words. Accessed 10 Mar. 2023.

51.   "What Great Listeners Actually Do." Harvard Business Review, 14 July 2016, hbr.org/2016/07/what-great-listeners-actually-do.

52.   Ibid.

53.   "Peter F. Drucker Quotes (Author of The Effective Executive)." Peter F. Drucker Quotes (Author of The Effective Executive), www.goodreads.com/author/quotes/12008.Peter_F_Drucker#. Accessed 31 Mar. 2023.

54.   Bennett, Roy T. The Light in the Heart: Inspirational Thoughts for Living Your Best Life. 2020.

55.   "19 Best ORSON WELLES Quotes - the Cite Site." The Cite Site, thecitesite.com/authors/orson-welles. Accessed 10 Mar. 2023.

56.   Chester, Tim. A Meal With Jesus: Discovering Grace, Community, and Mission Around the Table. 2011.

57.   Ibid.

58.   "Best and Funny Cooking Quotes to Get You Inspired." Hobby Sprout, 28 Oct. 2021, hobbysprout.com/quotes/cooking-quotes. Accessed 10 Mar. 2023.

59.   César Chávez Quotes (Author of Letters of a Nation), www.goodreads.com/author/quotes/345121.C_sar_Ch_vez. Accessed 10 Mar. 2023.

60.   "Employee Perspective: Martin Luther King, Jr. Day — Reflections on Greater Service | US Forest Service." US Forest Service, 15 Jan. 2021, www.fs.usda.gov/inside-fs/delivering-mission/excel/employee-perspective-martin-luther-king-jr-day-reflections. Accessed 12 Mar. 2023.

61.   Goff, Bob. Love Does: Discover a Secretly Incredible Life in an Ordinary World. 2012.

62.   James 2:16, The Message

63.   John 13:12-17, The Message

64.   ADOM :: Mother Teresa: The "Face of God's Mercy" in Our Lifetime, www.miamiarch.org/CatholicDiocese.php?op=Article_Mother+Teresa%3A+the+face+of+Gods+mercy+in+our+lifetime. Accessed 13 Mar. 2023.

65.   Caring. "The Best 18 Quotes From William Booth." Caring Magazine, 3 July 2020, caringmagazine.org/the-best-18-quotes-from-

william-booth. Accessed 14 Mar. 2023.

66.   Spurgeon, Charles. Morning and Evening. Our Daily Bread Publishing, 2016.

67.   "EVANGELISM." YouTube, 6 Feb. 2023, www.youtube.com/watch?v=J_k4nEMnDUI. Accessed 9 Mar. 2023.

68.   Proverbs 11:30, New King James Version

69.   "The Salvation Army Emergency Disaster Services." The Salvation Army Emergency Disaster Services, disaster.salvationarmyusa.org/aboutus. Accessed 12 Mar. 2023.

70.   Acts 13:46, New Living Translation

71.   https://amp.cnn.com/cnn/2023/03/22/football/leandro-requena-goalkeeper-longest-goal-spt-intl/index.html. Accessed 9 Mar. 2023.

72.   "AZLyrics - Request for Access." AZLyrics - Request for Access, www.azlyrics.com/lyrics/arethafranklin/respect.html. Accessed 12 Mar. 2023.

73.   Website. "Jesus Told Stories to Make a Point." Pastors.com, 16 Feb. 2011, pastors.com/jesus-told-stories-to-make-a-point. Accessed 12 Mar. 2023.

74.   Gottschall, Jonathan. The Storytelling Animal: How Stories Make Us Human. 2012.

75.   James 1:22, New Living Translation